CW01218473

this book belongs to
....

KAZ COOKE

GIRL STUFF

for girls aged 8-12

Your real guide to the pre-teen years

VIKING
an imprint of
PENGUIN BOOKS

CONTENTS

Intro 1

Part 1: The New You

1 Body Changes 7

2 Getting Your Period 19

3 Hair & Skin 32

Part 2: Being Healthy

4 Move 47

5 Eat 52

Part 3: Family

6 Happy Families 65

7 Making a Family Better 72

Part 4: Friends

8 Making & Breaking Friendships 83

9 Beating the Bullies 91

10 Phones, Apps & Being Online 106

Part 5: Feeling Good

11 Confidence 117

12 Moods & Emotions 126

Fun Lists 135

More Info 154

Acknowledgements 168

INTRO

Hello, girl! Welcome to being a **girl** – well, all right, you've been a girl for a while now. This book is all about the stuff you'll need to know as you get a bit older. It will be **your friend** through the changes as you head towards the teenage years. And before you scream into a pillow at the word 'teenager', **don't worry** – you're still a kid. And that's exactly what you're supposed to be. (If anybody asks for your job description, say, 'I'm a kid!' Actually, if anyone asks for your job description, give them a hard stare and edge away.)

Step 1: get a pillow
Step 2: scream into it

Some body changes might already have started happening to you or to your friends. Or, maybe none of them have happened yet. It's always good to know what's coming, even if you don't know exactly when. Periods, body hair, pimples, mean girls, wanting to use phone apps to stay in touch with friends: this book is going to help you with **all of that stuff**.

Changes don't feel so freaky when you know that they **happen to everyone** and when you get used to them.

This book, **GIRL STUFF 8-12**, talks to you about all the things you might feel embarrassed to talk to anyone else about. (So okay, this book won't talk out loud, but that's good, right? You can keep it under your screaming pillow and always read it in secret if you want to.)

bounce!

This book covers a lot of stuff that you don't have to know all at once. You might want to read it from start to finish like a novel. Or, you can just check out the contents list and read what you want to know about, **a bit at a time**. Up to you.

People in your family and friends might think changes that happen to you are 'too early', or comment, and you might feel embarrassed. I *promise* you're not weird. This stuff happens to all girls, but bits of it happen at different times for everyone. Some girls get their first period at 9, some at 15. You can be very different to somebody else, and yet you're both still **normal**.

You're not becoming a whole new person in a whole new body – the 'new you' is still just you. And you're not 'becoming a woman', not for years and years and yeeeears. You're just you (yay), being slowly changed into a newer version of you. This book is about **how to feel okay** about changes, and **how to be friends with yourself**.

tHeRe aRe maNy kinds of famiLy...

There are some quotes in this book from real girls, which are from more than 4000 girls who filled out a quiz for me. Girls wanted to know about, or comment on, all sorts of things. Using their comments, and info from doctors and other experts, I wrote **GIRL STUFF: Your Full-on Guide to the Teen Years**, which is for girls aged about 12 to 18. This book you're holding is the *Girl Stuff* version especially for younger girls, the 8 to 12 age group. When you see this text **GIRL STUFF :Your Full-on Guide to the Teen Years**, it means there's more info on that subject to be found in the big-sister version of this book, when you're ready.

Ask a trusted adult in your life if you need more info (Mum, Dad, an aunty, an uncle, a grandparent, friend's mum, school counsellor or librarian...) Right near the back of this book there is the More Info sections: one for you, and one for adults. There are great lists of fun books, movies and TV series, too.

So dive in, anywhere you like, and start finding out about Girl Stuff!

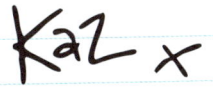

Kaz x

PART 1

THE NEW YOU

1. Body Changes 7
2. Getting Your Period 19
3. Hair & Skin 32

1
BODY CHANGES

So, Mother Nature can be a bit of a pain in the butt. Your body needs to make all sorts of gradual changes for you to grow up over the next few years. Some of those changes are already programmed into you as a baby, just waiting to happen. And the changes tend to happen way before you're an adult. It's like making all the preparations for a party a few years before the guests are even due to arrive.

Time for a change

The changes of 'puberty' can start anytime really between the ages of about 8 and 16. Nobody gets all the changes at the same time, or even in the same order. The changes include growing hair in unfamiliar places, getting a period every month or so, changing body shape and feeling new emotions. All that will be explained in this book.

Luckily, the various changes happen gradually over a few years. And no matter when it starts or how many of the changes have happened – you're still a girl. So, it's time to smooth out any worries and answer all those questions you might have. Let's get down to it.

Reasons you may not want to change

'Puberty' can sound freaky and scary before you go through it. 'Puberty', and 'adolescence' are just words used by doctors to officially name the normal development of a girl human. (Or boy human, but we're not talking about them right now.) The changes to your body – and your mind – can be confusing or annoying if you don't understand them, or you don't feel ready. Here are some of the common worries:

It can seem gross at first The changes can freak you out when they're new, but pretty quickly you just get used to having a period every month, or growing breasts, or getting taller, and you don't really think about it any more.

Grow UP? I'm not going to!

Some people won't shut up about it or refuse to talk about it at all Sometimes parents or friends comment on your changes. This is because adults and friends got used to you being little. They might say, 'It's too early. You're too young.' Remind them that it's obviously the right time for you. Show them bits of this book, if you like. In fact, I'll just do a quick bit of shouting on your behalf, so you can show them this next paragraph:

It's good to have somebody to talk to about it If you can't talk to your mum, try your big sister, dad, aunty, cousin, older friend, teacher, school nurse or counsellor, local doctor or friend's mum. This book should also answer most of your questions but it's always good to be able to talk with a real person who you can trust. (I mean, I'm a real person but I can't hear your questions from this distance, not even if you stick your head out the window and shout.)

> ## Attention, adults!
>
> What is happening to me is . . . completely NORMAL! Please be supportive and respect my PRIVACY as well as my need for information. No family member should be allowed to tease me, comment about my body or bang ON about it. That is all.
>
> Some adults have forgotten what it's like to go through the changes, so they say thoughtless things. And some other people just behave in a mean way, and might tease you about having breasts or otherwise getting bigger. People who tease are usually just thoughtless, or immature, or they are trying to draw attention away from their own worries and changes.

You feel like you're the first, or the last to go through the changes, or the only one going through it. You're not, though it can totally feel that way. You won't be the first or the last to go through every stage: things even out in the end. But sometimes you might feel like the 'odd one out' in a group of friends.

Why does your body change?

The changes happen because eventually you'll be a young woman capable of having a baby. Of course, you're not ready yet to even think about that – but Mother Nature is, as already mentioned, a bit bonkers. She wants to get all her homework done years early. So your body will start making more of various hormones, which are natural chemicals in your body's system. These hormones 'tell' the body to make its changes. Hormones are also found in your brain and contribute to changing your moods.

What's going to happen?

It can feel like your body is doing all sorts of weird obvious stuff on the outside. But most of the changes are ones you can't see: invisible, natural changes in hormone levels inside your body are making the outside changes happen. At first it seems like it's all imposed on you, and out of your control. You can feel like you don't know your body.

Such a big change happens to everyone – twice in their lives. You can't remember the first time because it was way back when the baby-you changed into toddler-you. The pre-teen and teen-years changes are just as necessary. They're totally norrrrrrmal.

You'll get bigger

You might get taller steadily through the pre-teen and teen years, or have a few growth jumps or one big growth spurt. Some girls grow several centimetres in a year. The time of quickest growth is often around 12 or 13, but that's not true of everyone. (Adults who haven't seen you for a while often sound *amazed* that you're taller than the last time they saw you; you'd think they would have got used to the idea by now. It's a bit like saying, 'Oh my GOD, the sun has come up again.')

Your hands and feet are the first to grow bigger, then your arms and legs, and then your spine gets longer. Your muscles get bigger and stronger. You don't see it, or even need to think about it, but inside, all your internal organs are also growing.

By the time you're as tall as you're going to get, at the other end of your teens, your skeleton will be double the size it is now. The rest of your body has to grow to keep up with your skeleton. Changing size can affect your sense of balance, and make you feel awkward or clumsy for a bit while you get used to your new self, but you'll adjust quickly.

> **FACT**
>
> Anything you have two of will be slightly different sizes to each other: this includes hands, feet, breasts, ears, the lot. Because you're paying such close attention you can think this is obvious, but nobody else would ever notice.

You'll get curvier

Over time, your breasts, hips and thighs will probably get bigger and rounder. Some girls will become curvier than others. Girls often worry about their tummy 'sticking out' but this bump is really common. It's normal to have either a flat or a rounded tum. Some girls will stay lean and not very curvy, even when they're fully grown – and that's fine, too.

'At first you think you're weird ... but really you're just like everyone else.'

Sarah

You'll get fluffier

By the end of your teen years you'll have:
- underarm hair
- pubic hair, which grows between your legs and on the pubic mound – the bump at the front below your tum
- leg hair that's more noticeable
- hair on your forearms (below the elbows) that also may be more noticeable
- perhaps some extra hair here and there.

(Also see the Hair & Skin chapter, coming up.)

UNDERARM HAIR IS USUALLY PRETTY SHORT

You'll get leakier

By the time you're a young woman, your skin and hair may become oilier, and you'll sweat more. I know this seems random at first, but you just get used to it because it's normal. Just as the first sign of your first period is usually seeing some blood on your undies, on some days when you don't have your period you might see some clear or whitish stuff on your pants. All of this is totally (all together now . . .) *normal*, and is explained in this chapter, coming up.

You might get moodier

One of the changes that hormones can make is that you have more extreme emotions. And as you get older, you'll have more responsibilities and things to think about at home and at school, and you'll have more complex feelings. You can feel sad, angry, weepy or wildly happy

> 'When I was first developing breasts and hair I was VERY self-conscious about it and DIDN'T want it to happen, but then I got used to it. But I remember it was hard getting used to it.'
>
> **Megan**

without exactly knowing why (see the Feeling Good section, later on). Some girls get crabby or emotional and teary before their period. Annoying! But also annoyingly NORMAL. Did I mention the thing about you being normal?

The order of the changes

Here's the order that the changes usually go in, taking about 4 to 6 years to get from little-girl body to full-on young-womanly one. But remember, the order can be different for everyone, and that's okay, too.

The secret stage

This usually happens at some point between the ages of 7 and 11. Internal organs of your body, including the ovaries, start getting bigger (more on those dear little ovaries later!). Your body sends hormone messages triggering other changes to happen.

Your hands and feet could get bigger and you could get taller (obviously this isn't so secret).

The bosom stage

Breasts usually 'start' anytime between the ages of 9 and 14. First you get 'breast buds', a hard little lump under each nipple. Usually this happens in one breast before the other one – could be the right or left. Months or even years later, the nipples seem to have pushed out a bit, so your chest is no longer flat, and your breasts start to grow. You can also have an all-over growth spurt during this time, getting taller and bigger.

The pubic-hair stage

This usually happens a little while after the budding-bosoms stage. (About one in five girls gets some pubic hair before she sees any bosom action, which is also,

THE NEW YOU ☀ body changes

you guessed it, *normal*.) The first hairs start out fine and straight and then might go curly. Some girls start getting wisps of pubic hair as young as 7 or 8. Eventually, you'll probably have a 'map of Tassie'– shaped 'triangle' of pubic hair.

The period stage

Usually about a year or two after the first sign of bosom business, you'll get your first period. Lots of girls get it when they're 12 or 13, but thousands of girls get it earlier or later (anytime between 9 and 15). This means some girls get it in primary school, and some in secondary school. Somebody usually feels odd because they're 'first' or 'last'. But they only feel odd because they don't know the thousands of other girls who are experiencing the same thing.

Get your mum or another trusted adult to organise a check-up for you with a doctor if your first period hasn't come before your sixteenth birthday.

Some pubic hair is sproutier than others

The underarm & leg-hair stage

This usually happens any time between the ages of 10 and 16, which means the average at about 13 or 14. The nipple area will also develop, and inside you, your body is starting to get its rhythm to do all the silent, invisible hormone messages it sends so that you have a normal period about once a month.

The you-got-it-all-going-on stage

Usually by about the age of 16, your breasts and body hair have 'finished' growing, and you're getting near your adult height. Your period comes about once a month.

For info on body hair, see the Hair & Skin chapter, coming up soon.

What to say to rude people

I don't know why some people say whatever stupid thing comes into their head. But here are some suggestions of things *you* can say to make people realise they're out of line, and that they should shut up. I know it's hard sometimes to say something back, 'specially if it's to an adult. Part of growing up is realising that not all adults are smart or nice or know what they're talking about. If necessary ask your mum or dad to step in for you and say something to any relatives and other grown-ups who've forgotten their manners.

Also, if it helps, you could 'say' some of the things on this list of suggestions silently, to yourself. Or practise some of your own 'retorts' to use.

'Ooh, you have put on weight.'
'Yes, that's what's supposed to happen.'

'Oooh you're changing shape!'
'My mum says it's rude to comment on other people's bodies.'

'You're getting boobs!'
'You do realise you just said that out loud?'

'You're becoming a woman.'
'Nope. I'm not even a teenager yet. But if you really think I'm grown up, can I borrow your car?'

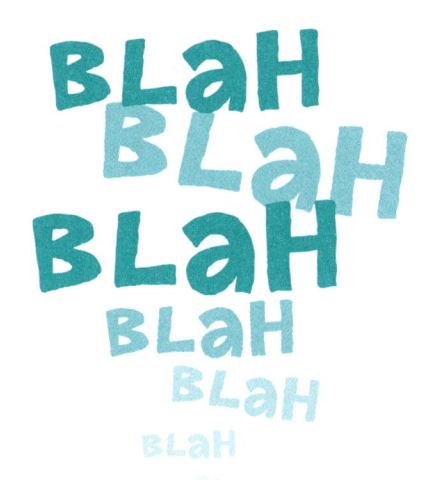

For general mean teasing, start with rolling your eyes and ignoring it, and if it continues, move on to asking for help from an adult if you need to. There are more hints about this in the Beating the Bullies chapter of the Friends section.

Breasts

Bosoms, boobs, bazoombas: call 'em whatever you like (but maybe not norks, jugs or rack). Once they start growing, breasts usually take 3 to 5 years to get to their final size. The point of breasts is to make milk, if you ever need them to, to feed a baby. (There's no milk in your breasts now.) (Or Milo.) (Sorry. Shouldn't have mentioned the mad idea of Milo coming out of bosoms. Am now horrified and have to lie down for a moment.)

Nipples

Nipples, the pointy bits of your breasts, have teensy-tiny holes, too small to see, like a sprinkler system so the milk can come out. Each nipple is in the centre of a coloured area technically called the areola, but honestly, I have never heard anyone say that word out loud and I'm not even sure how to pronounce it. Arry-oh-la, I think.

Nipples can sometimes get erect – harder and pointier. This is perfectly normal. (NORMAL, I TELL YOU!)

Innies and outies Some girls have nipples that always stick out. Some have turned-in ones, called inverted nipples (which are also normal). Inverted nipples sometimes pop out and say hello, especially if they're cold.

Ouchy ones Sometimes tender new nipples get sore from bouncing around and rubbing against your clothes. You can wear a firm-fitting crop-top or even a bra under your clothes to stop them bouncing so much. You're most aware of your breasts when they're 'new'. They may feel fuller and even a bit sore before your period.

> 'I woke up one morning and I swear my boobs just grew over night.'
>
> **Amy**

body changes ☀ THE NEW YOU

Breast size

Your breasts will probably start and finish growing at different times from your friends'. Most people have one breast slightly larger than the other. And they might grow at different rates.

Some girls worry that their bosoms aren't growing fast enough or big enough, or that they've happened too fast and become 'too big'. If any teasing goes on, remind yourself that girls with big breasts get teased about theirs, girls with small ones can get teased about it, and girls with middle-sized breasts get teased about something else or are told their breasts are too big or too small.

Getting teased about your breasts doesn't tell you anything about your breast size, it just tells you that the brain of the person teasing you is WAY TOO SMALL.

Initially, growing breasts is a bit of a shock. In the beginning they feel new and alien, even though they're part of you. And then you just forget they're there. Later in life, some women refer to their breasts fondly as 'the girls', whereas other women would no sooner name their bosoms as their ankles. It takes all kinds in this world – bosoms and people.

Do you need a bra?

Hundreds of millions of dollars are spent each year on ads telling you to buy bras. And they're not cheap. Girls only need a bra or firm crop-top when their breasts become big enough that it's uncomfortable or hurts when you're doing bouncy things such as exercising, dancing or playing sport. If you don't mind a bit of bouncing, then you don't need a bra. If you do feel you need one, get your mum or a friend's mum to help you work out how to get the right size for you.

'As the years go on, you get more and more used to talking about things like that.' **Bianca**

Downstairs & outsidey bits

Okay, we're talking about the In Your Underpants department. People have so many names for these parts, including vagina, genitals (pronounced jenn-ah-tals), girly-bits, front-bottom or even hoo-ha. (I know. Hoo-ha! Bizzare, and yet fun. I might start saying 'hoo-ha' more often when I'm not even talking about the underpants department.) There's more info on your insidey bits when we get to the Periods chapter.

Feel that soft, plump, roundish area at the top of where your legs meet, up front? That's your pubic bone covered by a little 'pubic mound' of nice, soft plumpness. This mound is where your pubic hair is going to be or has started already. All girls and women have this little bump.

It's harder to see what else is going on down lower, between your legs, although you can get a small mirror and use it to see what that looks like, if you want to.

The technical terms for the soft, folded areas are the vulva and labia, but you don't have to look, or need to look if you're not interested. It's just good to know. This area surrounds the opening into your body called the vagina, which we'll concentrate on a bit later. (I don't mean we will all have to concentrate on our vaginas with frowny expressions on our faces. I mean I'll be explaining more about vaginas in the Periods chapter.)

There's also a much tinier, cute little round bump hidden away among the folds between your legs, at the front end, called the **clitoris** (pronounced klit-or-iss). This is the most sensitive part of your body. One day, it will come in very handy but for now, if you want to know more about all that, and more details about your own lovely body, it's all in the big-sister book to this one, GIRL STUFF: **Your Full-on Guide to the Teen Years**.

Right. That's enough of the hoo-ha for now.

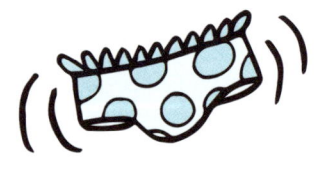

GETTING YOUR PERIOD

Be careful where you put your adhesive strip...

2

Why do you get a period? Because even though you don't need all the baby-making equipment inside you yet, your body is getting ready years early, just in case. And your body is sorting itself out so it works properly every month of your life that you *don't* have a baby. (Which as you can imagine is a lot of months!)

What triggers a period?

Various insidey bits of you act together to make a period happen every month or so, and they include:

Ovaries

These are two little glands that are originally the size of an almond, and grow to about walnut size in your teens. During pregnancy they will be the size of a fruit-and-nut chocolate bar. (No, I made that up.) You've got two, one on each side and above the uterus (we're getting to that). It's the ovaries that make the main female hormone, which is called oestrogen (pronounced east-ro-jen). The ovaries send the oestrogen around your body in the bloodstream.

Each ovary contains thousands of tiiiiny eggs smaller than this full stop. The eggs have been there, lurking near your stomach, keeping quiet and just hanging out, since you were born. Now, the hormones your body makes send messages to tell one egg each month to get released. The egg pops into a little nearby tube and tootles downwards verrrry slowly (up to 3 days to go a few centimetres!) towards your . . .

Uterus

Also known as the womb (pronounced woom to rhyme with room). The uterus (pronounced you-ter-us) grows from about the size of a thumb when you're little, to (look out, another fruit-and-nut comparison) a small pear. A hollow, upside-down little pear. If you ever have a baby in there, the uterus will grow bigger to keep the baby snug as it grows, and then it will shrink back to little-pear-size afterwards.

Every month the uterus builds up a new spongy, comfy layer of thick blood on the walls inside it, in case you have a baby (which of course you won't at this stage). So each month when your body realises that it isn't pregnant, the nice, comfy layer on melts away, and out it comes as blood – tada! – from your . . .

> 'It's much less exciting once it actually happens to you. I can't believe I was so worried that it would never happen!'
> **Gillian**

Vagina

Yes, indeedy, I know you've heard this word. Heading down from the bottom of the uterus is your vagina (pronounced vaj-eye-nar). This is a stretchy, hollow tube that leads straight down to the middle opening between your legs. This middle opening is between the front opening for wee to come out, and the back one for poo.

So once a month, during a period, a small amount of period blood trickles down from the uterus, down the inside of the vagina and out of that middle opening between your legs.

What to expect from a period

The first time it happens you might become aware of a wet or sticky feeling, or without warning you'll just suddenly see the bright-red period blood on your undies when you go to the loo. If the blood has dried out a bit, it can look browner. You can use pads that stick firmly onto your underpants to soak up the blood (more on pads coming up).

How often does a period happen?

A menstrual (pronounced men-strewl) period, which is the technical term, usually lasts 4 to 6 days. About a week after your period finishes (although it can be shorter or longer), another egg is released from an ovary and the whole palaver starts all over again. This is called the menstrual cycle, if we must. You get your period around every 28 days.

How much blood comes out during a period?

The actual amount is very small. Your whole period, over several days, adds up to about 2 tablespoons of runny red liquid. Some girls will bleed less than this and others more, and some have some clots amid the blood, which look a bit clumpier, more like jam. This is just some of the comfy uterus lining that's a bit more stuck together, and nothing to worry about.

There's usually more blood coming out on the first day of the period, then it gets less and less and finally fades to nothing. More than two-thirds of a period's total blood usually comes out in the first 2 or 3 days.

Does period blood smell?

Nobody will know you have your period unless you tell them. Think of all the women and girls in the world, each having a period once a month, and you never knew.

Period blood does have the very teensiest of odours, but nobody else can smell it because you change pads and tampons every 2 to 4 hours during the day and wash every day. It's only 'old' blood that tends to smell noticeably.

When to get ready

Because most girls get their first period anywhere between the ages of 9 and 15, most girls are always ready because they carry some pads in a special pencil case or make-up bag. You can keep one in your school bag, and one at home. You can ask your mum or school nurse, or a friend's mum, to help get this together.

> **FACT**
>
> **Period Problems** Get your responsible adult to take you to the doctor, or see the school nurse or if you had a period every month for a while and it's stopped, or if the bleeding is in some way not normal for you, or if it goes on for longer than 7 days or you get pre-period symptoms that really mess with your moods, or you feel cramping pain that gets in the way of enjoying life. Everything's probably fine and there's likely an easy way to avoid the hassle. Don't suffer in silence.

Period tracking

If you want to, you can use a diary or calendar, or anything – the back of an old lunchbag stuck on your bedroom noticeboard – to track when your period's due to happen. If you have a regular period, you'll know roughly when to expect the next one. Many girls have longer or shorter times between their periods than the average, which is about 28 days after the last one started. (The first day blood appears is known as 'Day 1'.) A lot of girls have their first couple of years of unpredictable periods and then settle down to more regular ones.

> **FACT**
>
> **Periods (mostly meh)** There's nothing magical, especially spiritual, shameful, secret or unclean about periods. They don't happen when the moon is full, and girls living in the same house don't always have their period at the same time. If they do it's a coincidence. Some old-fashioned attitudes about periods come from people who don't even understand why a period is happening, or from books written by men who didn't understand periods, hundreds of years ago.

Pre-period hassles

After a while you might start to recognise when your period is on the way. Known as premenstrual syndrome (PMS), in the few days before a period you could feel:

- tearful
- clumsy
- cranky
- having breasts and/or tum that feels bloated.

How to fight PMS

- To help reduce the bloaty feeling drink plenty of water and cut down on dehydrating salty foods and caffeine (not only in coffee, it's also found in chocolate, colas, energy and guarana drinks). This will make you wee often, which is a good thing.
- To stop fuller, tender breasts feeling sore, try a firm crop-top or bra.
- To keep your energy level, eat something yummy and healthy between meals, maybe a small handful of nuts or some vegies or fruit.

Period pain

Some girls don't have any pain for the first few years of periods. Period pains are sometimes called cramps, because along with the ache or pain is also a squeezy feeling, usually in the first day or so of the period. That's because the uterus actually *is* squeezing a bit, trying to help the blood slide out and down the vagina. It's saying, 'Goodbye, goodbye, hurry up, out you go.'

getting your period ☀ THE NEW YOU 25

FACT

Herbal palaver Don't take any 'natural therapies' or other suggested remedies for period problems without talking about them with your family doctor. It's important to get a diagnosis of any problem, and know what treatments are best for you.

Stuff you need for periods

Otherwise known as 'feminine hygiene products', for gawd's sake, pads and tampons are the small, disposable items we use to soak up (absorb) period blood. You can buy them at supermarkets, pharmacists and convenience shops.

When they're just starting periods, most girls try pads first because they don't feel ready to use tampons, which are pushed up inside the vagina. Using a tampon, by the way, doesn't make any difference to whether or not you are a 'virgin'. Only having sex changes that. Using tampons is safe and has no effect on your 'fertility' (ability to have children later).

Most girls don't want to use tampons for their first few times, or years, or ever. It's a totally personal choice. Companies now sell packs of smaller tampons and pads for younger girls or women with smaller bodies.

Especially during the first day or two of a period, a pad or tampon might take in all the blood it can absorb within a couple of hours. That's why you change them often. At your age you probably don't need to use 'super-maxi' or 'maxi' or 'heavy flow' tampons or pads. Some girls wear a bigger, 'overnighter' pad in bed when they have their period as they'll go for several hours without changing it.

'Girls find it hard to talk about things like this. Even though we are all going through the same thing you still feel a little uncomfortable. Now my girlfriends and I, we joke about it. We are so over it!' **Leisl**

THE NEW YOU ✻ getting your period

FACT

Absorbency Most tampons and pads have non-dangerous chemicals in them to help absorb blood. If a pad or tampon is advertised as 'natural' or 'just cotton', it may need changing much more often than the others.

Pads

A pad is rectangular, with curved ends (sort of like a surfboard – one of its nicknames). It has a sticky strip on the back: you put the sticky side down and press it onto the inside of your undies gusset (the bit that goes between your legs). (And yes, gusset *is* a ridiculous word. Carry on.)

When to change a pad On the heavier days of your period you'll need to change the pad up to every 2 hours, then later every 4 hours. This can be annoying if you get stuck without access to the loo for a while, say on a school bus trip. Use a bigger 'overnighter' pads for times like these. All pads or tampons should be changed after 4 hours during the day (whether there's much blood or not).

PADS of yesteryear were much more obvious...

1978

Types of pads Companies that sell pads would like you to wear a pad every day of your life so they sell more – but you don't need to.

- **Panty pads and 'liners'** These are not absorbent enough to deal with the usual amount of period blood. Women sometimes use them for the 'clear' or 'white stuff', (explained later), which shows up midway between periods.

- **'Girl' or 'starter' pads** Pads for younger girls or women with small bodies and therefore smaller undies gussets. These pads are usually a narrower width so they fit better into the knickers without overlap.
- **Ultra-thin pads** These are very thin but have a lot of absorbency.
- **Regular pads** These are the most useful on most period days for most women.
- **Super, maxi, overnight, or night pads** More absorbent or thicker pads which soak up more blood.
- **Wings** Some pads have extra-sticky side panels called 'wings' that wrap around the sides of your undies. This is because your thighs will squish the pad in a bit at the gusset sides, and 'wings' help a pad stay wrapped around so the blood doesn't leak onto your pants.

> 'When I first got my period I noticed the pad so much and could feel it, I thought everyone would be able to see it: but no one can.'
>
> Jemima

A pad is very unlikely to unstick itself and come out – I think you'd have to be wearing a skirt, dancing, adjusting your undies, doing the splits and a triple-back somersault all at the same time. But do stick them on firmly in case of unexpected acrobatic dancing.

Tampons

A tampon is a super-compressed little roll of absorbent material. It has a rounded tip to make it slide more easily up into your vagina, and a very securely attached string at the other end, which you pull on gently to drag it out. Most girls don't start using tampons until they're more used to a regular period.

A tampon is less messy than a pad because it soaks up the blood before the blood comes out of your body. You can swim with a tampon in – you can't swim with a pad because it will swell up with water. Only one tampon should be used at a time.

When to change a tampon Like pads, tampons need to be changed every couple of hours, especially on the first day or two of a period. Four hours is your maximum. And once you've taken one out – even if it hasn't soaked up a lot of blood, throw it away and use a new one.

Throwing away pads & tampons
Don't put them in the loo as they can block the drain and cause the loo to overflow immediately and alarmingly. Throw them into the container inside the toilet cubicle; they're in most public and school loos. Or put them into the bin inside the toilet near the basins. It can be useful to carry a couple of little plastic bags just in case you need to wrap a pad or tampon up in toilet paper, then pop it in a plastic bag and keep it in your pocket or a bag until you can get to a bin.

Types of tampons
- Slim, extra-slim, super-slim, starter tampons
  These thinner-than-ordinary tampons are for young girls having their first few periods.

Toxic shock: a very rare illness

No tampon should be worn for more than 4 hours max or all night because of the very tiny chance of getting a rare bacterial illness called Toxic Shock Syndrome.
(It's so very rare it's less than a one in millions and millions and millions thing.) It can get worse if you're wearing a tampon. If you have a really high fever and dizziness, have the 'runs' (sudden urge to poo), severe muscle pain and headache and you're vomiting . . . *and* you're wearing a tampon, take it out. Those symptoms together for any reason, whether you have your period or not, mean you must go straight to a doctor. Tell the doctor you've been using tampons so they can rule out the syndrome. (Have I mentioned how incredibly rare it is? Alrighty then.)

'I was actually 9 ½ when I got my period.' **Janne**

- **'Silky' tampons** These have a coating so they can slip in, and come out more easily, and are also good for girls who are new to tampons. Often combined with 'slim'.
- **Light, regular/medium and super/heavy tampons** The first couple of days of a period are usually the heaviest, but young girls usually just need a 'regular' on any day.
- **Tampons with applicators** Each tampon has a small, disposable cardboard 'syringe' to push it up inside you. Creates extra rubbish, and not necessary.
- **Twinpack tampons** These can have one pack of super and one of regular tampons. The idea is to use supers in the first couple of days, then move on to the regulars. At this age, you'll probably just need all regulars.

Getting a tampon in for the first time If you don't fancy starting to use tampons, don't. When you are ready, have a go. It might take you quite a few tries to get it right. Wash your hands first. It's easiest for the first time if you lie on a bed with your legs open, or you squat, or you stand with one foot on the closed toilet lid or the edge of the bath. Follow the instructions on the pamphlet inside the box of tampons, and unravel the tampon string before you start so you can use it to pull the tampon out.

It takes practice to get to the point where you get tampons in and out without even thinking about it. Start with slim or silky tampons, as they're designed to glide in more easily. Don't worry if you fluff up the ends on a couple trying to get them in. Just chuck them away.

Try to relax (breathe in and out deeply a couple of times) when you're putting in a tampon, and always point and push it slightly towards the small of your back, rather than straight up towards your head. It's easier to get a tampon into a vagina that isn't dry, so it's easier when you have your period than when you're just practising. You can pop a bit of Vaseline on the tip when you're practising.

If it hurts when you're practising using tampons, try again with new ones another time – you can always use pads in the meantime.

How far up should a tampon go? A tampon also needs to be pushed a little way up from the entrance of your vagina, otherwise it'll be uncomfortable all the time. When it's correctly in place you can't feel it. (Sometimes when you're wearing a tampon the string will end up in a position that feels annoying on your vulva – the outside area around your vagina opening – you just need to get to a loo and move the string.)

You can't push the tampon in too far – you'll always be able to reach the string, even if it gets a bit bunched up just inside your vagina. Every vagina will stretch to firmly hold a tampon perfectly. Tampons can't go travelling and get lost, and they don't fall out.

Removing a tampon When you want to change a tampon, pull gently and firmly on the string. If your vagina is dry and there is hardly any blood a tampon might feel a little resistant, but don't worry – the string won't break, and the tampon will come out.

Your period kit

You'll soon work out what you need, but here are some suggestions of what to put in your special pencil case or make-up bag as your period kit:

✻ tampons and/or pads

✻ baby wipes for washing yourself (although toilet paper is fine)

✻ spare undies if you want to be extra prepared

✻ 2 or 3 folded-up small plastic bags

✻ 2 or 3 sandwich-sized brown-paper bags if you want to cover a see-through plastic bag.

eMerGeNcy PeRiod kit

Running out of pads or tampons

If you're caught short without pads or tampons because you've run out of them, or your period has come unexpectedly, you may be able to ask someone if they have a spare. At school try the school nurse or a trusted teacher. At someone else's house ask your friend's mum, or call/text your parent to drop off supplies.

Hiding bloodstains on clothes Sometimes a little bit of period blood can soak through to your outer clothes. If you have a stain that can't be privately or completely rinsed out, or you can't scoot home to change, here's what to do:

- Get a trusted adult to help you: see a school nurse or counsellor, or a friend's mum – they should be able to help you get sorted out.
- Wear a jumper or hoodie tied around your waist and draped down at the back to hide the stain.
- Adjust the long strap of your bag, if it has one, so that the bag sits over your bottom area until you make it home.

The best way to get rid of bloodstains is to avoid hot water or washes, or a clothes drier which can 'set' the stain, before the stain is out. Scrub with laundry soap and cold water, or use a soaking powder according to directions.

The white stuff

Once your period seems to be coming every month or so, at other times of your cycle you'll probably notice some clear or white stuff on your undies. When it dries it can look a bit yellow and dusty. This comes out of your vagina, and happens to us all (well, girls and women). At about the time the invisible egg is released, in between each period. Some women wear little pads so it doesn't get on their undies, but you don't need to. There's enough pad palaver to go on with during period days, really. I'm only telling you so you know it's all . . . NORMAL. As long as you wear new undies and wash every day you'll be fresh and clean.

3
HAIR & SKIN

Gorgeous Skin — Just spray it on! *Sadly not yet available...*

Big Fat Hair in a Bottle

Your skin colour and whether you get many pimples is mainly decided and programmed into you before you're even born. In the same way, your natural hair and eye colour is also a pre-packaged deal. You may have inherited the genes from your parents or your grandparents or from relatives even further back, on either 'side' of the family — mum's or dad's. (That's why you can have red hair even if your parents don't). There's much more on skin and hair in the teenage version of this book GIRL STUFF: **Your Full-on Guide to the Teen Years**, but for now, here's what you need to know.

Hair

Because everyone's different, there's an amazing variety of head hair. It can be straight, wavy, curly, black, brown, blonde, pale strawberry blonde, red, or iridescent purple or green, if you dye it. All these things (except the purple and green) were decided by your genes inherited through your parents.

A lot of palaver is written in magazines and on websites about hair and conditioner, and the TV ads are full of models waggling their heads around to show their shiny, bouncy, magic, slow-motion hair. It's all designed to trick you into swapping to their brand of shampoo. Please ignore the bouncy, slow-motion waggling ladies.

It doesn't really matter if it seems you're suddenly getting dirtier or 'oilier' looking hair: just wash it when you feel you need to (at least once or twice a week). Just about any shampoo or conditioner from the supermarket is as good as the next one. So it's fine to use any shampoo from a big bottle that does all the family. You don't need a fancy conditioner, either. Very often the discount shampoo and conditioner is on the very low shelves – so help with the family shopping and scrunch down there to find the bargains!

glossy hair model

Body hair

Every girl eventually has body hair. Fair-haired and fair-skinned people often have less noticeable body hair than those with darker hair. Some people, such as those of Asian heritage, have less than others. Others, usually much to their annoyance, have more.

Some of us have more noticeable hair on our:
- Legs, especially below the knee.
- Arms, especially below the elbow.

MORE ▶

THE NEW YOU ✳ hair & skin

- Eyebrows and 'sideburns'.
- Upper lip.
- Pubic mound and between our legs, and sometimes in a little line heading up towards the tummy button.
- Nipples: as you get older many girls get the odd hair growing around these.

me too

every Body Has HaiRy Legs

Why do people remove their body hair? Even though it is compleeetely normal for girls and women to have body hair, you can feel pressure to remove it. Millions of women never remove any. Some do because they think body hair should only be seen on men. Other women like the smooth feeling when the hair is gone (but not the stubble as it grows back from the very next day when you shave it, or the itches if they get a rash from waxing it or using a chemical hair-removing product). Sometimes removing body hair has a practical use – very hairy underarms get sweaty more quickly and can be more smelly than smooth ones.

But mostly, women remove their body hair because it's fashionable in a lot of friendship groups and because people make big money from selling us hair-removal stuff. Companies that sell hair-removal products are trying to get younger and younger girls to remove their leg and underarm hair so they start spending money earlier.

Lots of girls don't notice their body hair after the first surprise of it visibly arriving, and are happy to ignore any leg, upper lip and underarm hair for the first few years, or forever. But a few girls still in primary school do get lots of bushy, dark underarm hair or very furry and dark leg hair that makes them feel upset, or they are teased about. It would be lovely to say 'just ignore that', but that might be no help to you at all. Most girls who remove body hair just do the legs below the knee and their underarms.

hair & skin ✸ THE NEW YOU   35

So if you really are being caused big problems by body hair, and if it's much less hassle to remove it than to keep it, ask your mum, a friend's mum or aunty to help you decide what to do.

If you are going to shave any of your bits, like underarms, you need to use a non-drying soap or foam to put on the area first, and use a sharp disposable razor (one that's only been used a few times). And be gentle and careful. Otherwise you'll end up getting a pimply rash or little cuts where you've shaved.

Upper lip If you have dark skin, any hair above your upper lip will probably be invisible to others anyway. A solution to make it 'disappear' if you have pale skin is to dye it blonde using body hair or facial hair bleach from the pharmacy (chemist) or supermarket. Never do this by yourself as it's complicated – ask a trusted adult to help you. Shaving upper-lip hair is no good, because it can cause a terrible rash, and will quickly re-grow into a spotty 'stubble'. Another solution is to pluck out the hairs that look obvious with tweezers, but remember, most people probably don't even notice what you're staring at super-close in the mirror.

Pubic hair If you've got some pubic hair and you're worried about a few straggly bits that might show when you're wearing bathers, you can choose a style of bathers that doesn't show anything. Go for a 'boy leg' shape, a one-piece rather than a bikini,

you HAVE tiny HAIRS all oveR youR BoDy...

or a two-piece shorts-and-top style. You can also carefully snip the sproutier ends so they don't poke out, using mini nail scissors.

A very small number of grown women remove their pubic hair, but most don't. Hair removal is usually done in a salon shop by an assistant using a sticky wax to rip out the hairs by the roots – which really hurts and is expensive. A few women shave their public hair, which can cause itchy stubble, cuts and infections.

There's more about hair removal and shaping in the big-sister book, GIRL STUff: **Your Full-on Guide to the Teen Years**.

Skin

Looking after your skin can be much simpler than it seems. There are only two main things to know:

- **Keep it clean** Wash your face every night. If your skin has started misbehaving and seems oily and pimply, wash it every morning, too. Don't use soap or soapy facial washes, as these are likely to strip your skin of natural oils. Warm water and a face washer, or simple sorbolene cream from the supermarket, does the job.
- **Keep it fed** Eat healthy food, which will help your immune system and keep your skin and hair healthy, and drink plenty of water.

Allergies & skin reactions

All chemicals and natural products, even organic ones, can cause a reaction on some skins. Be careful about borrowing sunscreen and other skin products from other people, especially if you've had problems and rashes in the past. Even though a label might say 'chemical free', that doesn't mean it's 'better'. Nothing is really 'chemical free' – even water is technically a chemical, and some chemicals, like vitamins, are good for us.

Skin marks

Everyone has one or some of these: freckles, moles, birthmarks, skin-stretching marks, scars or other facial differences. Some are more noticeable depending on things like your family history, skin colour, and whether the marks fade over time. Some girls want to cover these with make-up, but most learn to embrace their differences and even make a feature of them.

Pimples & blackheads

Even though pimples and blackheads are assumed to be a 'teenage' thing, lots of girls get them before they're a teen. Once your invisible hormones start getting busy, they can cause visible effects, including breasts and pimples.

This might be the occasional blackhead (blocked pore) or pimple, a little red eruption or spot. Some girls feel miserable if they get lots of pimples. Doctors sometimes call pimples acne, pronounced ack-nee. Nobody has to put up with a terrible pimple problem; there are ways of getting help.

Lotions & potions

You don't need brand-matching cleansers, face-washes, toners, moisturisers or exfoliators. If soap seems to make face skin too dry, you could try an oil-free face wash. 'More expensive' hardly ever means 'better'. Don't buy any products with 'microbeads' as after washing down the drain they pollute the oceans and choke fish and turtles.

> **FACT**
>
> **Pimple truth** Getting pimples or blackheads is not your fault. You're not doing something 'wrong'. Pimples and blocked pores are caused by hormones. They are not caused by lollies, chocolate, sugar, greasy food, dirt, germs, or not drinking enough water.

What are pimples & blackheads? Pimples are little eruptions caused by hormones making your skin oilier, which in turn can create blockages in your pores (the little holes in your skin). This can cause irritation and inflammation underneath, and pimples to erupt. Blackheads are simply blocked pores – they're not caused by dirt being stuck in the pore. The stuff blocking the pore from the inside can look dirty because it develops a darker colour when it's exposed to the outside air.

Fighting pimples If you have started getting pimples and you feel your life is being badly affected, get your mum or dad to take you to a pharmacy. Ask for the cheapest version of a non-soap, oil-free face wash and a 2.5 per cent or 5 per cent benzoyl peroxide pimple cream (ask the pharmacist for advice). Follow the instructions for the pimple cream. If there's been no sign of improvement after 6 weeks, or the problem is upsetting, or if you and your family are prone to scarring, you need to see your family doctor. Tell your mum or dad to get a 'referral' from your family doctor to a skin specialist who will be able to prescribe you the right treatment. There's more detailed info on doctors' treatments for pimples in the big-sister version of this book, **GIRL STUFF: Your Full-on Guide to the Teen Years**.

'Natural supplements' from health-food shops, bought online or from naturopaths won't help stop pimples, and some could even harm you. Always talk to your family doctor about what you are taking.

Squeezing pimples Everyone says not to squeeze, and talks in hushed and horrified tones about scarring and bacteria, but don't be frightened, sometimes you need to gently 'pop' one. Remember, the body is trying to get the gunk out because of the natural-forming bacteria underneath, that's why it's come to a yellow head.

You can gently remove a 'head' that's ready to pop. Wash your hands and your face first. Prick the yellow 'head' of the pimple with the end of a sterile needle or pin. But don't squeeze hard; if it doesn't pop with the tiniest of pressure, stop. Otherwise, tampering can cause more redness, bleeding or a little bruise.

Covering up pimples Any foundation make-up or 'cover-stick' used to colour over pimples should be oil free and matched to your skin colour, otherwise you just replace red spots with other non-matching coloured spots.

Pimple scars Scarring is more likely if you can't stop picking at or fiddle with pimples. But 'blind' pimples, the sore red bumps which don't come to a yellow head on the surface, can also cause scars. Scars can be very hard to hide or remove once they appear, so it's better to prevent them. Anybody can inherit skin that's more prone to scars, but it's more common in Asian skin.

Skin colour

All skin colours are beautiful. Your skin colour is decided before you're even born – and depends on whether your parents and ancestors were pale folk from Southern Europe or the Arctic Circle, or traditionally from Africa, Papua New Guinea and Aboriginal communities, or the Pacific Islands, or India, Pakistan and Sri Lanka, or near the Mediterranean Sea, or Asia, or South America. Or wherever.

In some places and friendship groups, girls want to use a fake tan to look darker. And in other countries or groups, girls consider using bleaching creams to make their skin lighter. This is sad, and is also sometimes dangerous, as apart from the expense, some of those creams and lotions can cause rashes and, in the case of bleaches, even scarring.

Sun & your skin

Protect your skin with sunscreen. This will mean you have far less risk of getting skin cancers (and extra wrinkles) as you get older. Use a sunscreen with a 30+ SPF, which stands for sun-protection factor. It doesn't need to be a higher number like 50 or more, or an expensive brand. A waterproof one is best even if you're not going swimming. More hints on staying safe in the sun are in *GIRL STUFF*: **Your Full-on Guide to the Teen Years**.

hair & skin ✸ THE NEW YOU   41

Make sure any gloop that goes on your face, like a sunscreen, doesn't clog pores (look for labels saying 'non-comedogenic', 'non-acnegenic' or 'oil free').

Tans 'Getting a tan' from the sun is dangerous and can damage your skin and even, in later years, cause skin cancer. Fake tans are popular

fake tans can look a bit carroty…

Getting the D you need

A shout-out to girls with dark skin or who wear hijabs and other covering clothes: you need to get extra Vitamin D, so that means more sun exposure when you can. People with dark skin take longer than pale folk to absorb Vitamin D from the sun – if you have very dark skin (from an African heritage, for example) you almost certainly shouldn't wear sunscreen or school hats in the playground. And girls who usually wear scarves, veils and clothes that cover their arms and legs, you probably need to uncover and get some extra sun when you can. (You still need to be careful not to get sunburned). If you live somewhere that's mostly cold and cloudy, try to get more sunlight on you in winter, especially if you have darker skin. If in doubt, ask your doctor, because you might need to take a Vitamin D supplement (pills), but your doctor needs to set a special dose for you that might be different to the adult dose on the bottle.

because companies advertise them and give them away free to celebrities. A fake tan is just a dye that is rubbed, sponged or sprayed onto your body.

We've all seen those celebrities who have overdone it and look like a beaming, gigantic, orange carrot wearing sunglasses. Some performance sports require you to use fake tans for special events, which is bonkers. It would be much more interesting, if we have to change colour all over, to pick one like lime green.

Sweating

Changing hormones means you get more sweat glands on your body, including under the arms and between your legs, and your feet. Have a shower every morning or every night once you've started going through pre-teen changes. And wear underarm antiperspirant, too. Antiperspirant (which some people call deodorant) helps to stop too much sweating, which can get smelly during the day. Use a roll-on so you don't inhale the particles from the spray ones.

How much you sweat is another thing that depends mainly on your inherited genes. Some people just sweat less because they're from a non-sweaty family.

Body piercing

You might already have your ears pierced. Because of the dangers of infections that can make you very sick, make sure you talk to the responsible adult in your life if you want to have it done. Any piercings should be done with new equipment (not used ever on anyone else) and properly sterilised. Piercings without a parent's permission are illegal if you're under the age of 16 or 18, depending on where you live.

Temporary tattoos

Real tattoos are deliberate scars that are made more obvious by adding indelible ink. They last forever but can fade, stretch, or sag. They're illegal if you're under the age of 18, in most areas of Australia. Some holiday destinations and stalls at festivals and fetes do 'henna' or other temporary body and face painting or pretend tattoos. You can also buy little kits or packets that put temporary dye or a design sticker on your body. The chemicals in some of these dyes can cause severe allergic reactions in people and in some cases it has resulted in scarring. You need to be sure that any face paint or 'temporary tattoo' is safe for you.

PART 2

BEING HEALTHY

4 Move 47

5 Eat 52

4 MOVE

Physical activity, whether it's a team sport, dancing, walking the dog, or dancing with the dog during netball is good for you. It makes you feel happier, keeps your body in good nick, gives you more energy, and helps you have a good night's sleep, fight off more germs, and make new friends.

Exercise

The point of physical activity, also called exercise, is to feel great and stay healthy. It feels good because your body is doing what it's supposed to – moving around, pumping blood around your body, getting oxygen in and out. Exercise strengthens your bones and muscles. It can make you feel stronger, happier, braver and calmer; the way you feel after a really good laugh.

What happens if you don't exercise

If you don't do any physical activity you'll become unfit and more tired and probably feel more unhappy. Being idle, still or sitting all day can make it harder to fight off the germs that cause colds and other illnesses.

What sort of exercise is best?

Whatever suits you, makes you huff and puff a bit, and is fun. It can be a team sport, or nothing to do with rules and competing. It can be mucking around in the park, or running at the beach, or walking the dog or having a crack at canoeing. And my favourite kind: dancing in the lounge room (or on your bed!). (Shoosh: don't tell your parents I said that!). There's a list of girls' favourite sports and activities coming up.

move ✱ BEING HEALTHY   49

The amount you need

You should get a total hour of physical activity a day. It's something to aim for, not a rule to get upset about. (Also, you should have less than a total of 2 hours a day looking at screens (TV, computers, phone, game consoles and other devices). No, really!

> 'I always feel better after I exercise!'
> Jharna

And while you're at it...

There are a few other smart things you can do to stay healthy while you're moving about: wash your hands before eating and after using the loo, don't chase lions, and brush your teeth twice a day. You should have a family doctor your parents take you to see if you get sick or injured. And you need to be up to date with all the childhood immunisations, including the ones for girls aged 10 to 13, which will protect you through your life against certain forms of cancer.

don't worry if you step off the path occasionally...

BEING HEALTHY ✳ *move*

Stuff girls do for fun and exercise

abseiling ✳ aerobics ✳ aikido ✳ aquarobics ✳ archery ✳ **athletics** ✳ Australian Rules footy ✳ badminton ✳ balinta wak (Filipino stick fighting) ✳ ballroom dancing ✳ **baseball** ✳ basketball ✳ beach volleyball ✳ belly dancing ✳ bobsledding ✳ bocce ✳ bodyboarding ✳ bodysurfing ✳ boogie boarding ✳ bowls ✳ building a tree house ✳ building fences ✳ bushwalking ✳ canoeing ✳ **capoeira** ✳ cardio boxing ✳ cardiovascular exercises in gym class ✳ carrying, not pushing, groceries ✳ circus skills ✳ cleaning vigorously ✳ **climbing trees** ✳ contemporary dance ✳ cricket ✳ croquet ✳ cross-country running ✳ cross-country skiing ✳ curling ✳ cycling ✳ **dance lessons** ✳ dancing on your bed with the door locked ✳ delivering newspapers or pamphlets on foot or wheels ✳ digging holes and planting trees ✳ diving ✳ **dog training** ✳ elastics ✳ fly fishing ✳ **Frisbee** ✳ fruit picking ✳ gardening ✳ getting up out of the chair ✳ gliding ✳ going the long way round ✳ golf ✳ gym machines ✳ gymnastics ✳ handweights at home ✳ hapkido ✳ hiking ✳ hiphop dance ✳ **hockey** ✳ horseriding ✳ hula hoop ✳ ice hockey ✳ ice-skating ✳ in-line skating ✳ Irish dancing ✳ **javelin** ✳ jazz dancing ✳ jogging ✳ judo ✳ jujitsu ✳ jumping ✳ karate ✳ kayaking ✳ kendo ✳ kickboxing ✳ kite boarding ✳ kite flying

yoga...

move ✦ BEING HEALTHY 51

✦ **lacrosse** ✦ Latin dance ✦ **lawn bowls** ✦ leaving the train/tram/bus early and walking the rest of the way ✦ line dancing ✦ long jump ✦ lunchtime walk ✦ **marching** ✦ modern dance ✦ mustering cattle ✦ netball ✦ orienteering ✦ Paralympic sports ✦ PE classes at school ✦ **petanque** ✦ Pilates ✦ playing catch ✦ playing sport with little kids ✦ playing the drums like crazy ✦ power walking ✦ **pretend boxing** ✦ pushing a pram ✦ quoits ✦ refereeing: the power! ✦ riding my bike to school ✦ rock climbing ✦ **rollerblading** ✦ rowing ✦ rugby league football ✦ rugby union football ✦ running ✦ running upstairs ✦ salsa dancing ✦ scuba diving ✦ **shooting hoops** ✦ shot-put ✦ skateboarding ✦ skiffle boarding ✦ skiing ✦ skipping rope – on your own or in a team ✦ snorkelling ✦ **snowboarding** ✦ soccer ✦ softball ✦ **squash** ✦ stacking shelves at work ✦ stair climbing ✦ stationary bike class ('spinning') ✦ stretching ✦ surf lifesaving ✦ surfing ✦ swimming ✦ swing dancing ✦ synchronised swimming ✦ tae kwon do ✦ **table tennis** ✦ tag ✦ **tai chi** ✦ taking the stairs, not the lift ✦ tap-dancing ✦ tennis ✦ touch football ✦ training ✦ **trampolining** ✦ trapeze ✦ treadmill walk or run at home ✦ tree planting ✦ tumbling (acrobatics) ✦ TV games like tennis you can do by yourself ✦ using a swing ✦ underwater hockey ✦ vacuuming ✦ volleyball ✦ walking dogs (part-time job) ✦ **walking with Mum** ✦ weight-training machines ✦ whitewater rafting ✦ windsurfing ✦ **woodchopping** ✦ wrestling ✦ yachting ✦ **yoga** ✦ Zorro-style fencing with swords (well, nobody said that but I had to have a Z).

There are lots more ideas for exercising and sports in **GIRL STUFF**: **Your Full-on Guide to the Teen Years**.

5 EAT

Yummo. Eating good food helps keep you healthier, happier and brainier. Because you're growing all the time (even when you don't notice), and you're getting bigger bones and you need to 'go up a size' several times in the next few years, you need regular meals and lots of good food.

Healthy eating

Every day you should eat lots of vegies of different colours (different colours means you'll get the different vitamins and minerals you need). The 5 colour groups are blues and purples, yellows and oranges, reds, whites and greens.

And nope, you can't just eat chips and pretend that's all the 'vegetables' you need! You also need to eat real fresh fruit every day – not roll-ups or fruit-flavoured drinks or yoghurts. You also need foods every day that have protein (meat, beans, cheese, milk or nuts and some other stuff) and grains (such as rice, bread and pasta).

Eat food as close to its original, natural self as possible. That means have a fresh apple, not diced apple in syrup bought in a tin, or a fruit-flavoured gel or strap bought from the supermarket. Most food in tins or in packets with flavourings and stuff added to it is called 'processed', which means it has less healthy vitamins and minerals, and probably has added or created sugars and salt or other additives that you don't need. (But frozen vegies are good for you!)

spinach, pumpkin, mushrooms, grapes, banana, plum

mix up your COLOURS

FACT

Tricky labels 'Organic' or 'Natural' label options aren't always the healthiest – they might be full of salt and sugar. And 'natural' may just be a slogan to distract you. Arghh!

Breakfast

Breakfast is important! Always have breakfast. Did I mention the BREAKFAST? It helps you last until lunchtime without feeling cranky and fuzzy in the head. Wholemeal and seedy bread, and oats (like porridge) are better for you than the cereals you get in big packets, because a lot of them have lots of added sugar and have most of the good stuff taken out. Other good stuff to have for breakfast includes cheese, nut-spreads on toast, a banana, a smoothie and boiled eggs. (You can get these boiled the night before so they're ready to go from the fridge in the morning. Just don't get the boiled eggs mixed up with the raw eggs or there could be a total lunchbox *disaster*.)

Vegetarians

Girls who don't eat meat need to have a carefully planned diet with foods that specifically help them to keep growing their brain and body properly. There are some vitamins and minerals that are hard to get just by eating non-meat foods.

If you want to be a vegetarian, you need to talk to your doctor or a qualified dietician first, and talk with a parent about how to get enough nutrition, and the specific vitamins you need. As a pre-teen and then a teen, you will have different nutritional needs from adults – you need to eat more protein and iron, and vitamin B12. Almost all info for vegetarians is for adults. (The reason why I say to get info from a 'qualified dietician' is that legally, anyone can call themselves a 'nutritionist', but a dietician is a special title for those with recognised medical training.)

> **FACT**
>
> **Healthy snackery** Good munchies include carrot and zucchini sticks, home-made popcorn without butter or butter substitute, fruit salad and cheese. Good lunches are a wrap with some salad and protein such as cheese or tuna, and a piece of fruit.

Drinks

Make water your main drink. You can fill a water bottle from the tap at home or school if you want to have a drink with you. Milk with added vitamin D once a day is a good choice, too.

Fizzy drinks, also known as soft drinks or soda, are not good for you. Bought fruit juice, or juice and cordial in boxes, isn't a great choice for you either. That's because the fruit juice hasn't got enough fibre in it, and the fizzy drinks and cordials have so much sugar in them they're like liquid lollies. These drinks, as well as 'diet' drinks, most of which have acids in them, can also put holes in your teeth.

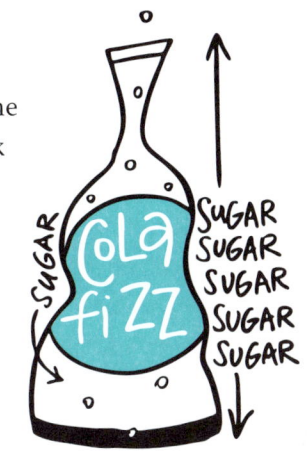

And say your biggest NUP to 'sports' or 'energy' drinks, even if you feel tired or you play sport. They are no good for kids. They contain high levels of caffeine and way too much sugar to be healthy for you. The same goes for guarana drinks, all cola drinks, coffee and cups of tea. Chocolate also has caffeine in it, which is why a little bit is okay but a lot can make you run around like a maniac for no good reason and then not be able to sleep properly (I'm looking at YOU, Easter Bunny).

Water is what you need when you're thirsty. And it's free.

Cakey things & takeaway or fast food

The high-sugar, high-salt, and high-fat foods are things like cakes, muffins, some breads, chips, and fast-food like drive-through or shop hamburgers and fried chicken. It's okay to eat this stuff occasionally.

Food allergies & intolerances

Food allergies mean that if you eat or come into contact with what you're allergic to, it can make you very sick, or even be life-threatening. Some people have allergies to peanuts and other nuts, shellfish, eggs and other foods. A food intolerance means you find it difficult to digest or process a certain food, and if you eat it you might feel sick or get a rash. For some people, 'trigger' foods might be dairy food, or a certain natural or added chemical. Everyone's allergy or intolerance is different, and needs to be respected.

Suspected food allergies and food intolerances need to be medically confirmed by a doctor, not a parent or natural therapist. You might need to go to an allergy specialist to work out what is causing the problem. If you just stop eating one kind of food because you suspect an allergy, you can cause another health problem. Sometimes tummy aches and other problems are not caused by an allergy, but by another illness that isn't obvious, or by feeling worried, or by eating too much, or even eating a bit of something you haven't eaten for a while.

Symptoms of food intolerances or allergies can include rashes, a runny nose, nausea, farting, diarrhoea (not so amusingly pronounced 'dire rear') or constipation (not being able to poo for a while), a bloating feeling, tummy ache, vomiting, wheezing or, in rare cases, a life-threatening allergic 'anaphylaxis' shock reaction (it's pronounced ann-affel-ax-is).

If you do have a food intolerance or allergy, the adults in charge of any situation will need to know about it. You may have to be strong and smart about how you eat, and be confident to say no, speak up or tell an adult to 'speak to my mum/dad/doctor' if they don't understand or don't believe you.

Healthy size

Many people assume that thinner always means healthier, and that dieting is the best way to do that. That's just so not true. We're about to find out why – and there's more on this in the big-sister version of this book, GIRL STUFF: **Your Full-on Guide to the Teen Years**.

To be healthy, you need a body that lets you do all the physical activities you need and want to, and is able to fight off illness. You need lots of energy, and some body fat, and you don't need to know how much you weigh. There's no one exact healthy or perfect weight to match your age group or height. There's no magic amount of kilos, or clothes size, or any number that you need to aim for. As long as you eat lots of good, healthy food and do lots of physical activity, you'll be somewhere within an okay, healthy weight range for you.

Being under or over that healthy weight range could cause internal organs to become under strain, and make injury and illness more likely.

> 'Being healthy isn't always about what size you are or what other people think. Being healthy is when you feel comfortable with yourself, eating right, and feeling fit.'
>
> Lana

Body types

After you're fully grown, your size can be affected by what you eat and how much you move your body around, but your shape will always be essentially the same. It isn't based on what you eat, your star sign, your blood type, or any other ancient made-up system, or on the latest theory from someone trying to sell a stupid new diet book. That's all piffle. We inherit our body shape and potential height from our relatives, through a combination of genes. You may not look or be anything like your sister, or your mum. You may take after Great Aunty Nuala who you never even met. Two people can eat the same food and exercise in the same way but still have different body shapes and sizes.

We all need body fat

We female folk can get a wrong idea about what's normal and natural when it comes to fat. We need fat! Fat is not the enemy. To be properly healthy, girls need to be putting on body fat as well as muscle and more height as they get older. It's a natural part of becoming a young woman. It's healthy for fit, gorgeous, normal girls and women to have body fat. It doesn't mean we're *too* fat.

Speaking in averages, a 10-year-old girl needs and has 10 to 15 per cent more body fat than boys of the same age. A grown woman has 10 to 30 per cent more fat than a man.

This girly padding that happens as we grow towards being a woman is mainly around our breasts, hips and tummy. It's there because we need it to have regular periods, and to help our bodies in case we ever want to have a baby. If our body fat falls below a healthy level it can result in all sorts of problems, ranging from from lifeless, dull hair to easily broken bones.

Being thin is okay too

You don't have to have big bosoms or wide hips to be a real girl or woman. A lot of girls are genetically programmed to be small and thin or tall and thin all their lives, before as well as after the changes of 'puberty'. Naturally thin girls are just as beautiful as girls with more curves.

You are you-shaped

Don't take to heart any mean or thoughtless comments about your shape and size even if they're from your mum or someone else you love – such comments happen because of ignorance about weight and eating, or because of the other person's own problems or bad feelings.

It's okay to be rounded, and tall, or short, or thin. There's no 'best' shape or size for everyone. Just lots of different ways of being gorgeous. Including yours.

> 'Diets are stupid and make you fat and feel really crap about yourself!! Never go on one, ever!!! Diets are not fun, and anyone who tells you they are has problems and you should refer them to a counsellor.'
>
> Emily

Why 'diets' suck

'Diet' can be such a confusing word. It even gets adults all mixed up. Some people use the words 'a good diet' to mean having good eating habits. But 'a good diet' can sound like 'going on a diet'. And 'going on a diet' is bad for you and can damage your body and mess with your mind. And foods and drinks labelled 'diet' and 'low fat' are usually full of too much sugar, which causes weight gain.

You might hear adults talking about diets as something positive they should do, and see magazines, and apps and even people you talk to, banging on about 'going on a diet'. But it's still a bad idea – especially for kids and teenagers.

The reasons that some adults want to go on diets are complicated, but mostly they are trying to 'lose weight'. But dieting is their enemy. Ninety-nine people in every 100 who go on a diet will lose a bit of weight, but then put it all back on again. When a person 'diets', the messages to their brain about hunger get confused. Their body thinks it's starving so it sends more messages to the body about eating more, thinking about food all the time, and conserving energy for a starvation period. All of this is bad for your body and your mind.

Fasting

Fasting – not eating all day – isn't healthy for kids. 'Detoxing' diets are not needed by adults or children. Don't take part in not eating for charity marathons; you can show your support in other ways.

Some girls are asked to fast at specific times for religious reasons. Most girls won't be asked to begin this tradition until they are anywhere from 12 to 20 years old, depending on a definition of 'maturity' which varies between families, and churches, synagogues and mosques. Most schools have a policy about this settled with input from parents and local religious leaders. Many families and religious schools observe Lent, Ramadan or Yom Kippur not by requiring school students to fast, but instead to help donate their time or collect money for the needy, and to pray with their families.

Before any kind of fast, you should check with your family doctor: if you're not physically and mentally ready to fast then it's okay not to. At your age you have a special need for daily foods with protein and calcium and you need to drink water throughout the day. Many older kids do a version of religious fasting in which they have less than usual, but have snacks with them in case they feel faint or really need to eat.

Diet horrors Dieting can cause illness, hunger, trumpety farts, tiredness, crabbiness, forgetfulness, headaches, muscle cramps, constipation, weak bones, a lack of vitamins and minerals which makes you more likely to get sick, skin problems, sadness and bad breath. Dieting can set you up for a lifetime of feeling out of control, and sad, bad and mad about food.

> 'Diets are wrong. A healthy eating scheme and exercise plan are much better. It gets me REALLY p . . . off when my grandmother tells me about diets.'
>
> Sofia

eat ✱ BEING HEALTHY 61

> **FACT**
>
> **Sum total**   Changing your 'diet' so you eat more healthy things = good. Going on a 'diet' to try to lose weight = bad.

'Going on diets' can muck up the proper messages to your brain. The messages are things like when you're hungry, when you're full, what you need to eat, and whether you feel like you're in the right weight range for you.

damn

poot

Diets make you farty

PART 3

FAMILY

6 Happy Families 65

7 Making a Family Better 72

Families come in all sorts of shapes and sizes. It might be Mum and you. Or Mum, Dad, Granny, and 3 brothers and sisters. Or Dad, Dad's boyfriend and his kids. And the ferret. If you're lucky, your family will be lovely and full of cuddles and people who spend time listening to you and helping you.

6
HAPPY FAMILIES

What makes a happy family?

Every family faces certain challenges, and probably every family isn't as happy as they might seem to be. But some families are definitely happier than others. Happy families seem to share some of the same elements; not every family can achieve these, but working towards them can make family life happier.

In a happy family people tend to:
- love each other and show it
- like and respect each other
- communicate honestly and openly with each other
- spend time together
- solve problems together
- get through bad times together
- not have serious stresses such as mental or physical illness, drug or alcohol abuse, war or a history of distressing events
- have an okay financial situation so that they are not worrying about money all the time – this is not necessarily about how much money a family has, but its attitude to money
- be willing to find ways to get on better together.

> 'We've had some great and awful times. But we've always pulled through them together. No matter what happens I know they'll be there for me. I love them.'
>
> Cassie

Getting on with a parent

If you get on with a parent everything is easier. Letting them know you well is an important part of this. Tell them what you think about, what your hopes and worries are. Tell them when you find something difficult, when you're trying your best, when you are happiest. And tell them that you want them to be proud of you.

Try to be honest. If you let them know how you feel they won't have to guess (and maybe get it wrong): 'I guess I feel angry because I really, really wanted to go.' Let them know that when they start panicking or yelling as soon as you tell them worrying stuff (such as someone offered you drugs) it makes you feel you don't want to tell them anything.

You don't have to tell a parent everything – you are entitled to your privacy and thoughts – but it will help you to get on better if they know how you think and feel.

It also helps if you make an effort to understand where *they*'re coming from (which can be hard to do if your parent or parents are away from home a lot or otherwise busy or distracted).

How to get to know a parent

- Offer to team up with them for a walk some days, before or after their work. It will give you a chance to chat.
- Help to make the evening meal, and sit down together to eat it.
- Take the time to get to know the parent you spend less time with (even if you have to do this by message, emailing or texting).
- Go on family outings and holidays (you can trade these off for other occasions when you want to do something else).
- Show support by offering to help them with extra chores when they're going through a rough time.
- Go to their work or to sporting events if they want you to: this makes it more likely they'll return the favour when you need it.

'I can talk to my mum about anything and I know she won't judge me.' Hailley

- Let them know that you appreciate what they do for the family and that you're proud of *them*.
- Accept apologies from them as you would want them to accept yours. You're old enough to know that your parents aren't perfect: they make mistakes and can handle things the wrong way.
- Ask them what rules they had when they were around your age.

Getting to know your parent better

Ask them:
- What they loved when they were your age
- What naughty things they did when they were kids
- What makes them happy
- What makes them sad
- What they'd most like to do in life
- What they have to do at work, and whether they like it.

Brothers & sisters

How you get on with your siblings (brothers and sisters) can depend on your ages; personalities; whether one needs more health care than the others; and whether you are seen as equal and individual (you may not be treated the same, but you can be treated with equal fairness and love).

Good things about brothers & sisters

- They understand where you are coming from.
- They can be an ally against your parents.
- They can be loyal friends when you need them.

I used your lipgloss

SIBLING CRISIS

- They can give you a feeling of belonging.
- You can share lots of secrets and memories.
- Younger ones look up to you.
- Older ones do some of the hard work with your parents on gaining freedoms before you have to.
- You don't usually stay mad with each other for long.

Annoying stuff about brothers & sisters

- They can seem to be the favourite.
- You may have a personality clash.
- They may take your stuff.
- They're in 'your' space (or face).
- People assume you're the same.
- People expect you to 'follow in the footsteps' of an older one.
- People expect you to take responsibility for the actions of a younger one.
- People assume because of your position in the family you'll have a certain personality.

Different family combos

Most kids think their family is 'normal', whether their dad is a trapeze artist in Bolivia or a plumber, and their mum wears a turban with a feather or is the Minister for Education. Just because your family is 'normal' – and most families *are* normal in their own, weird way – that doesn't mean it's like anybody else's!

Sole-parent families

For some or all of your life you may have known or lived with only one parent. It may be because your other parent died or can't come to this country; but sometimes it may be because one parent decided from the start that they didn't want to be involved in a family, or they drifted away after a separation or divorce.

Some parents don't want to be in their kid's life. This is never the kid's fault. Some adults can't handle the responsibilities of bringing up children or never learnt how to make a good family. It's okay to be angry about feeling let down by one of your parents, but it helps to talk to someone about it. Be proud that you're part of a successful team with one parent.

Being adopted

Finding out suddenly that you're adopted can be confusing. It's usually easier when your adoptive family is open and honest about it from the start.

When you're older, you might feel you want to find your birth parents. Many people decide to wait until they're 18 to meet their birth parents, as it can be a big, emotional grown-up thing to do. Some people feel it's a difficult thing to raise with their adoptive parents, and don't want to hurt their feelings.

But there are agencies that can help you find your birth parents, and reunite you. They are not allowed to give your contact details to anyone searching for you until you give your permission.

Some reunions with birth parents are successful, and some aren't. There's a lot to think about, and no way to predict the outcome. You may want to have a continuing relationship, or you may just want to meet once.

Same-sex parents, grandparents & others

Some familes have two dads or two mums, or a creative combo that emcompasses the fact that one or more parents is gay. Lots of grandparents, aunties and uncles also fill the parental role, as do foster parents.

'Blended' or 'step' families

Most parents who separate will make new families straight away or within a few years by taking up with a new partner – and sometimes that partner has their own kids or will have a baby with your parent. So there'll be a 'blended' or 'step' family situation – with all kids living in the same house all the time or moving between their parents' houses.

Getting your head around the idea of a new family is a pretty big project, especially if it happens before you've absorbed the shock of your original family coming apart. Sometimes it's the upsetting point at which you really understand that your own parents will never get back together.

It can take time to adjust to a new blended family, both with your emotions (you can't just automatically love new family members) and practical stuff (such as suddenly sharing a bathroom with more people). It can feel like you have no control over who is in your family or where you go. Try to keep talking with your parent, and if you need to, pick a trusted relative or family friend to talk to about any worries. There's more on this in the GIRL STUFF: **Your Full-on Guide to the Teen Years**.

Also see Family Break-ups, coming up in this book.

blended family

7

MAKING A FAMILY BETTER

family Rules
1. no undies on heads
2. feed the ferret

There can be temporary problems or ongoing bad times in a family even if outsiders don't see what's going on at home. You can always find suport from people around you, even if your family isn't such a happy one.

Not-so-happy families

Every family has its tensions, its secrets, its roles for each member (the clown, the peacemaker, the naughty one), and some families are dysfunctional (don't work properly) and full of tension and strife. Many families, though, can learn how to turn fights and arguments between generations, or between siblings, into (reasonably!) calm discussions.

Taking the heat out of arguments

Perhaps your family can agree to a few guidelines that will help calm a disagreement. Here are some examples.

- Anyone can make an appointment to discuss something with another family member or call a family meeting.
- No interrupting. Everyone waits their turn to speak and listens respectfully.
- Nobody is allowed to end a discussion without hearing everything the others want to say – but a discussion can be suspended until everyone has calmed down.
- No shouting or insults.
- No physical hostilities.
- No pouting, sulking, flouncing, theatrical sighing or slamming of doors.
- Discussions must be conducted without sarcasm, mimicry or other meanness.

If it feels as if a discussion is getting off track, try to get the family to refer to this plan: somebody raises a problem, then everyone talks about their ideas on how to solve it and the possible drawbacks they see to each solution, and finally everyone agrees on how to go on.

Maybe you have a parent who is stressed ←

Tension breakers for yourself (& other family members)

Things get tough for everyone from time to time. Take time out to:
- Scream into a pillow
- Do something that makes you laugh
- Have a bath
- Go for a walk
- Chat to a good friend
- Dance madly in your room for 15 minutes.

Step 1: get a pillow

Step 2: scream into it

When a parent isn't there for you

- Ask for their attention, in a nice way. Try a suggestion like, 'Mum/Dad, can we do something together soon, such as make a cake/see a movie/play Frisbee?'
- Explain that you understand they're very busy, but you don't want to turn into one of those kids who only get attention when they do the wrong thing. That'll scare 'em.
- If they're busy, or in the middle of a temporary project, ask to make an appointment with them for an activity or a talk later on and stick to it.
- If they're always busy, ask them when they think that might change, or what you could do to help change it.
- Wait for the right moment to talk to them. Don't interrupt them when they're on the phone or in the middle of something else (including an intersection).
- Learn a few parent-friendly phrases such as 'I'd really like your advice', or 'I think you could help me with this', or 'Can I come with you and help?'
- Try a regular 'appointment' with a parent – such as Sunday brunch or a Friday-night walk.

When families change

Family break-ups

Lots of kids have parents who decide to separate or divorce (divorce is just the more legal and official version). Sometimes it's a shock to be told parents are 'breaking up'; in other families kids might suspect it for a while. Adults have usually thought long and hard about it before they've decided.

Some former partners stay friends, even taking holidays together as a family. In some families the parents don't love each other any more but they're always polite and never criticise each other in front of their children. And some unlucky kids (because it's never, ever the kids' fault) find themselves stuck in a breaking, or broken-up family in which the conflict, hurt or anger between them is so strong that the adults keep fighting and saying bad things about each other and continue to fight, or refuse to communicate.

If the adults can't agree on how to share the parenting and who should be with which parent at different times, there may be a hearing at the Family Court to decide. Each parent will say what they think should happen, and a judge will make a 'ruling' that the parents have to follow. The judge will make sure that each child involved gets to say what they want, too. Because the court's main aim is to do what's right for the kids, you may be asked to see a court worker, a trained counsellor, to talk about how things are for you and how you'd like things to be resolved. There is not enough money or staff available to the Family Court so sometimes there are long, difficult delays in getting a ruling.

Finding out why a separation happens

There are a lot of important things you'll probably want your parents to explain when a family separates or an adult moves out. Keep in mind that parents separating is never caused by their kids. It's something that happens between the adults. If it hasn't already been explained to you, choose a calm time to ask any questions, if you want to know the answers.

Your first question might be, why did the adults decide to stop living together? Parents may have decided not to discuss it with you because they're afraid it's upsetting, but maybe you want to hear the answers even so. You can say you just want a general answer, and don't want to hear details of fights or who-did-what-when.

You can quietly let your parents know that you don't want to 'take sides', or that you don't want to hear either parent say mean things about the other: that you don't want to pass on 'messages' between parents, they will need to 'talk' to each other even if just through texts and emails.

Speak up if you're not happy with the living arrangements they've decided on and you'd like to spend more or less time with a parent. You don't have to make a decision suddenly or quickly: you can just say how you'd like the arrangements to be for a month or longer, and then change them later.

Often after a separation or divorce one or both of the parents will have less money. One may give you presents and money to reassure you they still love you, but a parent who can't afford lots of presents still loves you.

Go easy on yourself as this isn't something you just get over immediately. Your parents are upset, and you're upset. You're not in control of the situation, and it's normal to have feelings of anger and sadness.

Good things to know about having separated or divorced parents:
- Your parents may not 'belong' to each other in the same way, but you will always belong to both of them.
- You have a right to continue to see both parents, and both sets of grandparents, if you want to.

Family abuse

In a family the abuse might be against a partner, the kids or the whole family. Physical abuse is often called domestic violence or family violence because it involves physical threats or injury. But emotional abuse can also be used in a family; for example, a mum might be controlled by the fear of her child being hurt, or a child controlled by the fear of their mum being hurt, or by cruel words.

Sexual abuse of children and teenagers also occurs within some families. The abuser can be a parent, a parent's partner, an uncle or grandparent, a sibling or another relative, a family friend (or a teacher, coach, religious leader or some other adult trusted by the family), who might:

- do things to the child or teenager's private parts, or make them do something to the abuser
- look at their private parts in a sexual way
- insist they look at pictures (on a computer, TV or somewhere else) that seem wrong and make them feel uncomfortable
- do or say something else that feels wrong or creepy
- make the child or teenager touch them sexually or have some kind of sex with them.

The abuser might say things such as 'It's normal', 'Don't tell anyone', and 'It's our secret'. Often they might threaten to hurt the kid (or somebody else), or to shame them if they tell anyone what's going on. Or the abuser might say that nobody will believe the kid if they tell. But there are people who can help you and make the abuse stop.

If you are being sexually abused you need to know that this is *not* a secret that has to be kept. No matter what they say:

- it's not your fault – it's never your fault
- it's against the law
- it's never normal or right

- and, no matter what they say, it's not your fault – by doing this to you they have betrayed your trust in them and that is very wrong
- you can get help and protection.

Sexual abuse can be confusing, especially when the person doing the abusing is someone you love or have been taught to obey. It doesn't happen because a person 'can't control their sexual urges', or because the way you look 'makes' them do it. You might feel guilty or ashamed, but you are not the person responsible for the wrong thing. The abuser knows what they are doing and has made a choice. You can get help and support to realise you don't need to be ashamed.

Legal rights of children & young people

All kids and young people have human rights. Australia signed the United Nations Convention on the Rights of the Child (CROC) way back in 1990, agreeing to its contents. The convention sets out and protects the rights of children up to the age of 18. Under it you have the right, among other things, to:

- freedom from economic and sexual exploitation
- have your own opinion
- education
- health care
- a safe place to live
- economic opportunity.

What to do about abuse in a family

It can be very hard to know what to do or who to trust after emotional, physical or sexual abuse. But you can go one step at a time, without anyone in the family finding out at first. In some families, people want to keep the abuse secret. You need to tell a trusted adult – perhaps another relative, a teacher or school nurse, a doctor, your friend's mum – or call a helpline. It is scary to take this step, but it's the first step to making it stop – and it must stop. If a friend tells you they have been or are being abused, you need to tell a trusted parent or a teacher, or help them to tell. It is not something that you can solve or make okay; it's a job for the right adults.

You can't fix this by yourself, but there are ways to make your life safe, and there are people who will help you: reach out to them.

More info on abusive families

These places will help with emotional, violent or sexual abuse.

Kids Helpline: 1800 55 1800
Free 24-hour counselling and advice: you can call without giving your name.

burstingthebubble.com
Info, advice and links on what to do about violence and abuse in your family and how to help a friend.

reachout.com
For teens having a hard time.

LifeLine: 0800 543 354
Anybody of any age can call, 24 hours a day, for free advice and help.

PART 4

FRIENDS

- **8** Making & Breaking Friendships 83
- **9** Beating the Bullies 91
- **10** Phones, Apps & Being Online 106

8 MAKING & BREAKING FRIENDSHIPS

Some days it seems what's happening with friends can take over your brain. Do you need a best friend? Are you in the right group of friends? How do you break up with a friend, make new ones, be friends online, deal with a bully, or stop yourself from being the mean one? Is it okay to lose a friend, even on purpose? (Yes!) Read on...

good friends can make you laugh 'til you cry...

Good friends

Having friends can make life so much easier and more fun. It means laughing so much you nearly wet your pants (or you actually do wet your pants – but enough about me). It means hanging out together, and having private jokes and memories. It means writing and drawing and climbing trees together, borrowing each other's stuff, hanging out together, being there to help each other through bad times, having someone you can blather on to about absolutely anything.

It's about having a safe place to go, except that the safe place is a person or a group of people. You might have different friends in different places, holiday friends, neighbourhood ones, school friends, new ones and old ones.

How to be a good friend

Good friends are reliably good company and share jokes and some opinions. But you don't have to agree about everything or have the same hobbies or favourite colour to be friends.

Real friends don't want to hurt each other's feelings and are not mean on purpose. Think before you say something: do you really need to say it out loud? If you do say it, will it hurt somebody else's feelings? If a friend asks your opinion, think of kind ways to reply that are also true. 'You're gorgeous, let's go and play ping pong' is a better answer than 'Yes, that is a bad haircut and you do look a bit like there's a beard on your head.' Both answers might be true but only one is helpful. Real friends will be sincere when they say sorry – and good friends will forgive mistakes and misunderstandings.

What makes a good friendship?

Some friendships are good for a little while, or even a long time, but then it's best to move on. Many girls find it too intense to have a best friend, or only one close friend.

> 'I just want lots of good friends, not a best friend.' **Maddie**

Real friends:
- genuinely like each other even if they don't agree on everything
- don't gossip about each other
- like doing some of the same things
- listen and try to understand each other's feelings
- stick up for each other
- are not mean or sarcastic to you
- treat you the same, no matter who else is around
- don't try to control what you say, wear or like, or who your other friends are.

a good friend doesn't blab your secrets

Choose your friends

Don't sit back waiting to be chosen. Your job is to choose! You're better off being on your own a bit more until you find a good friend, so wait for a good one. Don't just drift into a group because you've been chosen by someone who's too bossy, way boring or not very nice to you.

Sometimes you might take a fancy to somebody who doesn't want to be friends with you. That can be hard, but you have to move on.

Not everyone has to like you or be your friend. A couple of friends are enough.

Making new friends

Making new friends can be hard, especially if you're shy. If being shy is part of your personality, it's not something that you can or should 'stop'. (There's more on shyness in the Confidence chapter, coming up.) The most obvious

> 'Surround yourself by a good group of friends. They always see the good bits, the important bits.'
>
> Kat

FRIENDS — making & breaking friendships

place to make friends is at school, but there are plenty of other places too.

Making good friends takes time. Don't go telling people your deepest, darkest secrets when you first meet them, or asking them really personal things, as this could scare them off. ('Hi. Will you be my BFF which means forever and ever and ever, and can we swap underpants, what was your name again? Hey, where'd everybody go?')

> 'Kids can be so cruel, it's hard to remember you are beautiful. Surround yourself with positive, supportive people.'
>
> Maya

Where to look for new friends Is there someone you see around but have never got to know? Is there a girl in the school library reading a book you love? What about your local neighbourhood? Can you reconnect with kids from your area who go to different schools? How about cousins or friends of friends, or the kids of your parents' friends who you haven't seen for a while? Think about joining a local or further-away sports team, band, bushwalking club, filmmaking class, or circus-skills, art or martial-arts group, or finding classes or groups at community centres and local libraries near you.

making & breaking friendships FRIENDS

Groups of friends

Are you in a group which almost has an unofficial uniform (everyone has the same sort of haircut), and headquarters (hanging out at the same place each lunchtime)? A small friendship group might suit you – but it could also make you feel you're living in a little box. Instead, you could choose to be friendly with lots of people rather than joining one group or having one 'best friend'. There's more on 'fitting in', 'being yourself' and other elements of friendship, in the big-sister book GIRL STUFF: **Your Full-on Guide to the Teen Years**.

And then one day, I realised all the people in the 'cool group' behaved like chimps...

FACT

A friend is a friend Being friends with a boy, or a few boys, as well as girls, is perfectly fine. Some people might be stupid about it and try to tease you and stuff like, 'Ooooh, is he your BOYFRIEND?'. Just roll your eyes and ignore them. If they keep being horrible, see the Beating the Bullies chapter.

'Do something outside of school so you make friends away from your school groups and stretch your comfort zones.' Phoebe

How to fix a friendship

First decide if you really want to fix it or would rather it faded away. To fix it, spend a little more time together, ask the friend to your place, or hang out with them at school a bit more, and gradually you may find the friendship is back on. Sometimes it's just time going past that heals a friendship. Friendships can be up one week and down the next, or even on different days. If you need to apologise or ask for an apology, do that. And remember, you can't fix a friendship by yourself. The other person has to want to, as well.

> 'You need to surround yourself with people who love you and can keep you really positive about every situation you get in. They will keep telling you that you can do it and help you to become a strong person.'
>
> Chelsea

How to leave a bad friendship

It can feel messy and upsetting. One way to get through it is to keep reminding yourself what you want. This could be new friends who don't tease you, or some other friends who do stuff instead of just sitting around being mean about other girls. Any sadness and stress you're going through will be temporary, and your life will be so much better when you have drifted to another group or pal you feel more comfy with.

Doing the drift You can just let a friendship wind down by gradually spending more time on other things and with other people. Do other things at lunchtime and playtime for a while, even if that's being in the school library or joining supervised activities. Say your parents are making you do it, if you think that will help. You can slowly start to spend time with another group, or other friends.

> 'I have never really fitted into a particular group anywhere. I'm friends with lots of people in different groups.' Trudi

Peer pressure

'Peer group' means a bunch of people of similar age, or a group of friends. Your classmates and friends are your 'peers'. 'Peer pressure' is when other people try to make you feel that you should change your behaviour, your hair cut or what you wear, your religious beliefs, or your opinions.

Peer pressure can be:

- **Direct** Somebody orders you around and tells you to do something you know is wrong.

- **Implied** You know that if you don't wear what the others are wearing the 'head' of a group will be mean to you and others will follow that lead.

- **Manipulated** Advertising and other kinds of marketing of products can make you feel you need to buy stuff to be cool.

- **Internal (comes from within you)** If you feel unsure of yourself, you might copy others to try to 'fit in'.

- **Unconscious** Suddenly you realise everyone in your friendship group wears the same brand of shorts, or orders the same lunch.

How not to be controlled Always have a few good comebacks ready for when you're being pressured into something you don't want to do or say. I have lists of lots of ways to say 'no' to big things (like smoking or drinking) in the big-sister version of this book, *GIRL STUFF*: **Your Full-on Guide to the Teen Years**. In the meantime, read the Confidence chapter for hints on being yourself.

Stuck in the middle No friend should ask you to ignore another friend, or to 'take sides' in a disagreement. You have the right to stay neutral. You don't have to stop talking to one friend because another friend says so. You can say: 'I don't want to get involved', or 'I know you're hurt/angry/upset about this, and that's bad, but I won't ignore her.' You can also say, 'I think she said the wrong thing, but she said she's sorry, and I still want us all to be friends.'

> 'I made a pact and said that next school year I'm getting out of this group even if it means I'd be alone for a while. I made loads of awesome new friends and am really happy.'
> Katherine

BEATING THE BULLIES 9

The flipside of friendship can be meanness and bullying. When somebody targets you to be horrible, it can make you feel confused, angry, upset and powerless. This chapter explains why it's normal to have hurt feelings, and how you can get some power back to protect yourself and find new pals.

Meanness & bullying

Sometimes if you tell an adult about a kid being horrible to you, the grown-up will say, 'Oh, just ignore it'. Next time, ask the grown-up, 'Okay, tell me who was the mean kid in your year at school?' I'll bet they can remember the person's whole name and everything else about them even if they haven't been at school for 15 years. Adults sometimes need to be reminded that meanness that upsets you is always important. Grown-ups need to take your problem seriously.

Meanness can even come from someone who claims to be your friend. It's nasty to say something cruel to somebody directly. And it's also mean to make horrible comments 'behind somebody's back'. Meanness includes nasty comments, spreading rumours and gossip, whether it's online, on phones, or in person. We've all had it done to us. Sometimes we've even been guilty of meanness ourselves. But it's not okay to keep being mean. Continuing meanness is bullying.

Some adults say that being bullied is part of the 'real world' and that everyone has to put up with it at some time in their life and everyone survives it. But we all have the right to live without harassment and discrimination. No one deserves bullying, and no one 'asks for it'.

So what's the difference between meanness and bullying? Well, bullying is not just a one-off event. It's very hurtful, there's a deliberate intent to hurt your feelings, and it keeps going. It could be regular, often or constant, by one person or by a group of people. Bullying on phones or social media website pages can be called 'cyberbullying' – which just means it's done using electronic devices, not 'in person'. Bullying can make some people feel sad, angry, and even desperate.

But there are lots of things you can do, and help you can get to make it stop. If you're feeling in despair, go straight to the

'Ignorant guys/girls make comments about me being in a wheelchair… they call me a fraud.'

Kate

back part of this book, find the More Info page, and ring the Kidsline number.

Some people just stay nasty all their lives, so it's good to know how to deflect their meanness. (Because leaping at them from trees and trying to strangle them is apparently illegal. I checked.)

> 'I completely changed friendship groups, which was the hardest and best thing ever.'
>
> **Win**

So what is bullying, exactly?

All the things on the following list are mean. If they become repeated, ongoing or relentless, then it's bullying:

- nasty comments and insults
- teasing
- 'jokes' and hoaxes, such as telling you the wrong room to go to at school, or pretending to be somebody else online
- rudeness when you're talking (rolling of eyes, sighing, sarcastic comments, whispering, mimicking, mocking, or smiling in a mean way as if they're laughing at you)
- spreading gossip and rumours
- ignoring you or getting others to ignore you (I call this the 'freeze-out')
- intimidation – following you, looming over you, staring at you
- threats of physical violence or of telling secrets or lies
- sexual comments, rumours, insults or pornographic pictures shown or sent to you
- damage to your clothes or other things you own
- physical violence.

what if I beg?

How NOT to 'HaNdLE' Rejection

Being different

Being 'different' can make you feel like a target. So many kids hear, 'You're weird' all the time. (The smart answer to this, even if you just think it to yourself, is: 'You only think that because you're boring.') Mean people can be jealous, racist, otherwise ignorant or stupid, or just freaked out by anything 'different'. In the end, the joke's on them because everyone's different – and that's one of the joys of life.

Every single famous pop star, actor, artist and other interesting person has been told 'you're weird'. Your identity is precious. It could well be the thing that makes you famous, or just makes you fun to be with.

Differences can include skin and hair colour, ethnic heritage, language, disabilities, sexuality, interests, skills, hobbies, religion, even taste in music and clothes. The more you embrace your differences, the more successful and happier you can be.

You may feel you're not accepted in your family, school, friendship group or town. That doesn't make you wrong – it makes you special. And right now, there are others just like you, or who will understand you, in the same situation living in other families and schools and towns. And one day you will meet them all and have cake. Well, you'll meet some of them. And there'll definitely be cake.

> 'I worry that when I am myself my friends won't like me.'
> Smita

> 'You don't realise how much it hurts until it happens to you.'
> Lulu

The freeze-out

Nearly everyone is targeted by a freeze-out from a friend's group at least once in their life. Suddenly, everyone in that group starts deliberately and obviously ignoring them. It feels awful when this happens to you.

'It's harder to be nice, but more rewarding.' **Mary**

Of course sometimes it happens accidentally: for instance, people forget to save you a seat. But sometimes it's an Intentional Freeze-out. You know the kind of thing: people turn their backs or walk away when you arrive, ignore what you say, give you dirty or cold stares, make sure you catch them whispering about you. It's very immature of them, but it's still horribly hurtful and makes you feel like bursting into tears.

Usually, nobody will tell you why they're freezing you out. It can go on for a lunchtime, a day, a week, or in rare cases even longer. Of course all the time the group is careful not to let parents and teachers see what they're doing. What they're doing is bullying you. Sometimes I think girls do the freeze-out because it makes them feel powerful. Some do it because they've 'learned' at home in their own family. That doesn't make it okay.

The reasons for bullying

I get cranky when some teachers and parents say, 'We just need to tell the person who's bullying that they're hurting somebody else's feelings.' The problem with that is that most bullies KNOW they're hurting your feelings – and they don't care, or that's the result they wanted.

People being mean can be loners or part of a group. They can be someone your own age, or older, or sometimes even younger. Mean people can include your friends, a family member, a kid in your neighbourhood, a teacher or a boss.

In a way, it's important not to spend too much time wondering WHY you're being bullied. It's never your fault because even if you said something or did something you regret, bullying is not an okay response. The most important thing is that a bully should have to face consequences for their behaviour, so that it stops.

'I had this friend who was really mean. I was willing to do anything to make her think better of me. So I turned into a really mean person. I feel so bad.'

Lucy

But shall we have a quick look at possible reasons for bullying? All right, if you insist, here they are:
- The 'leader' of a group is testing her power by ordering meanness against you (possibly you have angered Her Majesty by being more interesting than her, or by standing up to her). (Her Majesty might be a boy instead of a girl, in which case he could be referred to in the comfort of your own mind as King Twit).
- Other kids in the group are 'easily led' by, or scared of the mean 'leader'.
- There's a rumour going around about you – it might be true or untrue.
- Some bullies are just unhappy and mean.
- The bully usually feels superior: better than everyone else.
- The bully usually feels inferior: not as good as everyone else.
- No adult has stepped in yet to demand that the bullying stop.
- The bully is bored and stirs up drama to entertain themselves.
- The bully is boring and unimaginative, and feels threatened by more interesting or clever kids.
- Some bullies think they don't have to face their actions if they're doing it online.

If you're being bullied, don't waste too much time asking, 'What have I done wrong?' It could be anything. Or nothing. Instead, ask yourself, 'How can I find some nicer friends?'

Bad excuses for being mean:
- 'I was just telling the truth.'
- 'I didn't do it on purpose.'
- 'I was just joking – they should get the joke.'
- 'Everyone does it.'
- 'They were mean to me so I was mean back.'
- 'It's what girls do.'

'I spread rumours I knew weren't true.' **Amy**

'I'm trying to be nice now and just being an all-round nice person to everyone makes you feel better inside.'

Amal

That last one's the biggest, baddest, excusiest excuse of all. Lots of girls and women support each other, as friends and in jobs when they're grown up. It's not fair or true to say that all girls and women are mean to each other and that's how it will always be.

The real reasons for meanness

Bullies and kids being mean probably each have a different reason for being horrible. That reason is really only useful to know if it helps to work out how to make them stop. Some kids don't care about other people's feelings, or make themselves feel more powerful by trying to control and boss around other kids. Some kids are not brave so they go along with whatever a bully says. Some kids 'learn' mean behaviour at home, and think that's how the world works. Some bullies think they can get away with being mean if they do it online, or somewhere that adults can't hear it.

If you're the one being mean

In the replies to the Girl Stuff Survey, about 70 per cent of girls aged 13 to 18 said they had been mean to somebody else, although many said they regretted it. Probably almost everyone has done it at least once: the important thing is not to get into the habit. Even if it has become something you do a lot, you can stop.

'I talked about people behind their backs and made fun of them to their faces, but as it happened to me also I realised I was really hurting people. I am now much more careful about things I say.' **Felicity**

Why you should stop being mean

Each time you're about to say or do something mean, think about it first, and stop yourself. If it's not something you would like to happen to you, don't do it to somebody else. Think about the good reasons not to:

- It's the right thing to do.
- You'll like yourself more, and so will other people.
- You won't have to feel guilty about it.
- Any text, message, posting or email you've written will be evidence against you – even if you used a fake name you can be traced.
- Companies who supply your connection to the internet and social media apps will cut off access and block accounts for being mean or bullying. In serious cases there can be a criminal charge by the police.

Speak up when it happens to someone else

Even if you don't like somebody, it doesn't mean they deserve to be picked on. If you're in a group when mean things are said, you can speak up. Say, 'I hate it when you're so mean', or 'I don't want to be part of this: see you later.' You can walk away alone or with the person who's being picked on. You don't have to be best friends with them forever – the point is to do the right thing at the time.

If you get mean texts or see mean posts, ignore them, or delete them if you can.

'I was in a group at school and thought everything was fine, then one day they all just literally stopped talking to me, and now they are talking to me again and I asked why but no one ever gave me an explanation.' Ruby

How to deal with meanness & bullying

Ignoring meanness is hard: it doesn't always make it go away, and it doesn't stop it hurting. Even if you walk away or don't show a reaction, inside you can still feel crushed or furious. And that's an understandable and normal reaction.

Sometimes anti-bullying tactics work, but sometimes they don't. Some will work sometimes, or on some bullies. (I mean, how can you 'avoid them' if they're in your class ALL day?)

Some ideas to try:
- Ignore them. Don't react, don't reply, look right through 'em, walk away. Feel free to smile silently, or roll your eyes.
- Be assertive: stick up for yourself.
- Imagine them standing there with a big dollop of dog poo or sloppy seagull poo on their head they don't know about.
- Confuse them. Sing loudly, recite poetry or comedy, shout: 'Yes, the lobster army is marching! To the barricades!' They'll say, 'You're crazy,' but then you can say, 'Ooh, woolly hats akimbo!' Bullies are often unsettled when confused.
- Stay positive: focus your mind on people who love you, good times you've had and all the things you like about yourself.
- Threaten to tell an adult. Tell the adult.
- Learn a self-defence martial art so you feel more physically confident about defending yourself against physical violence if necessary.
- Hang out in a group: several people against a bully can work.
- Tell the harasser in person, to stop. You might want to be with a parent or teacher when this happens, or get them to help you send a message in response to a rude or horrible post on social media. If it's on social media, block them if you can (see the online and phone stuff coming up soon).

> 'They call it being "brutally honest", but sometimes I feel that some comments should be kept to yourself.'
>
> Pip

- If an embarrassing photo of you is sent to other people or posted somewhere, get help to make sure it's taken down, and ask your parents to involve the school if necessary to stop it happening again. One photo, or one event doesn't define you as a person and it won't 'ruin your life'. Get help and support from friends, parents, trusted teachers or a school counsellor. You will get through this, and come out stronger with better friends.

Getting support against meanness & bullying

Asking for help isn't a sign of weakness: it takes courage. If the first person you tell isn't helpful, keep trying until you find someone understanding who can make things happen. People you might ask for help include: the person at your school in charge of doing something to stop online bullying and harassment; a parent, a friend's parent, teacher or school nurse, school counsellor, friends. Like any good detective, you need to build your case. Tell somebody on the day that meanness happens. Keep any handwritten notes or texts, store posts or take screenshots of mean messages. Don't keep reading them over and over – give them or show them to an adult and they can store them when you delete them. Show any obscene or horrible texts, website or email messages to a trusted adult.

Help from home Sometimes it's just helpful to talk about stuff that's annoying or upsetting, even if nothing actually gets 'solved'. Brothers, sisters, cousins, aunties, uncles and parents may be able to help you by sharing problems and talking things through.

In cases of ongoing meanness or bullying, ask a parent or guardian for help. Tell them there will be a school staff member who can advise them on this sort of stuff. A parent can also get help from their online service provider, which can investigate and shut down the bully's account. (There's a useful More Info for parents page towards the back of this book).

You can show this box to your parents or guardian:

> ## Attention, adults! BULLY ALERT!
>
> If your kid speaks to you about meanness or bullying, take it seriously. This is a mental-health issue. Your kid needs support. Speak to the staff member at school with responsibility for this and see the online and phone info coming up for more info on what to do to help.

Help at school Report the bullying to the school staff member responsible for bullying or social media (ask your teacher who that is, or ask your teacher for help). If they don't do anything about it that works, get your parent or guardian to ask the principal's office for a copy of the school's bullying policy. All schools must have one. If the school is dodging its responsibility, a parent can complain directly to the principal's boss, the education department in your state or territory.

> 'Despite the saying "sticks and stones may break my bones, but names will never hurt me" words hurt, equally as much as actions.'
>
> Jessica

Snappy comebacks

You can come up with your own snappy replies to mean comments, and practise so you can deliver them easily. If you can raise one eyebrow, or say 'Wow' with a level stare or a roll of your eyes, practise that, too. Here are some sample snappy comebacks:

They say: 'Can't you take a joke?'
You say: 'Can't you stop being mean?'

'It was just a joke.'
'Nope, jokes are supposed to be funny.'

'You need to toughen up.'
'I don't have to change because you want to be mean to me.'

'You're too sensitive.'
'I'm not oversensitive, I'm just over it.'

'Friends tell each other the truth and I'm your friend.'
'Doesn't sound like friendship to me.'

'I'm just telling you the truth.'
'No, you're just being mean.'

'Well, it's true.'
'Saying it's true doesn't make it true.'

'I'm just saying . . .'
'Try thinking before you do that.'

Take a break

As well as fighting back against bullies, you can get away and you can get a fresh start if necessary. Even small breaks and safe spaces from stress can be really useful.

- Don't keep being drawn back to people who are always or often mean.
- Use safe zones in a school like a patrolled area or the library.
- Walk home with an older sibling or other group of friends, or get a parent to come and walk with you for a while.
- If 'friends' are mean, it means they're not friends. Don't try to laugh it off or think it's normal to have hurt feelings.
- In some really bad cases, after you've tried everything else, you may be able to move schools and make a fresh start, if you can. This works wonders for some people.

> 'Ignore comments from those peers who don't have two brain cells to rub together: the majority of the "popular" people at school.'
>
> Jo

Change the feelings caused by bullying

Bullying can cause stress, fear, low self-esteem, illness, physical injury, loneliness and depression. But some of these feelings can be turned around, with practice. Instead of each of the common thoughts below, try the ones in bold.

First thought: 'It must be my fault somehow.'
More useful thought: 'No, it's not my fault.'

'It's never going to stop.'
More useful thought: 'There are things I can do to try to make it stop – and I'll start right now.'

'I have to face it alone.'
More useful thought: 'I need to talk to an adult who can help.'

'Nothing can help me.'
More useful thought: 'There are lots of people and strategies that can help.'

'Nobody likes me.'
More useful thought: 'I need to find some of My People. These are not My People.'

'I'm scared to go to school or where the bullies are, but I can't escape.'
More useful thought: 'I can escape: I need help to stop this, or to move to another school.'

'I feel rejected and depressed.'

More useful thought: 'I need to find some friends and get some help. I will start feeling better and be back on the way to happiness.'

'I need to pretend I'm fine and make lots of jokes.'

More useful thought: 'I don't have to pretend this is okay. It's not a joke if only one side laughs.'

'I should pick on someone else so that they do too, and leave me alone.'

More useful thought: 'I won't let them turn me into a mean person.'

'They make me feel ashamed of myself, my family and my culture.'

More useful thought: 'I'm proud of myself, my family and my culture. It's the bullies who have the problem.'

'I don't fit in anywhere.'

More useful thought: 'This is not a place where I would want to fit in. But there is a place for me where I can be different *and* fit in, and I'll find it. I am not alone.'

10 PHONES, APPS & BEING ONLINE

Most girls aged 8 to 12 don't need their own phone, and it's illegal for them to use 'social media'. But some girls seem to do nothing BUT stare at their phones. What's the deal? Here's what you need to know before getting a phone & letting loose online.

Girls & social media

You're not legally allowed to have your own social media accounts until you're at least 13. Even if your friends' parents have different rules, that doesn't make it okay. If you are reported to be underage to a social media app company, your account will be shut down.

Most girls don't get their 'own' mobile phone until they're 12 or older. Some girls borrow a family one on special occasions. But most 8- to 12-year-old girls go online in some way every week (this can include downloading or listening to songs, watching videos, playing games on a hand-held device, using social media apps, or searching for information for a school project).

'I didn't get a phone till I was 14 because I didn't need one, I just used Mum's.'

Hannah

As well as the upside and fun part of using social media and online games, there are some downsides, too. Some kids use social media and phones to say mean things, and to bully other kids. And there are some creepy adults who pretend to be kids online, or to find out where you live so they can rob your house or otherwise do something scary.

Some apps are dishonest, and are designed to sneakily get more money from your parents. Many apps and online sites are not suitable for kids, and have upsetting stuff on them. Be smart and avoid being a target for mean people, scams or creeps. Get help when you need it from a teacher or parent or another trusted adult who's already in your life.

It's time for you to tell your parents the rules! You can show them the list on the next page, which is what experts say parents need to know about social media:

15 things parents need to know about phones, apps & being online

1 Although some parents allow it, it's illegal and unsafe for kids under the age of 13 to have their own social media accounts.

2 Kids can be online using music-playing devices, mobile phones, 'tablets', any computer, game consoles, home TVs, most apps, and some other devices, including watches and some clock radios.

3 Parents must keep up with the fashions in new social media apps and platforms. The longer your kid stays off social media, the longer you postpone potential problems, and your own need to monitor it.

4 Apps and social media are only as safe as whoever has access to it, and that's everybody. Most apps aren't for kids. Apps and games can collect personal information, solicit money, and identify your kid's location. Strangers use various ways to con photos out of kids, and arrange meetings.

5 Anything that's posted online, even a family photo, should be considered 'public'. Its use and who sees it is out of your control. Kids need to understand this.

6 Kids under 13 should use their parents' email address. When a child gets their own, it shouldn't include their full name, year of birth, or reveal they're a child. Parents should monitor any account. To avoid 'viruses' or 'malware', parents should teach kids to delete any email from anybody they don't already know, *without opening it or clicking on any link in it.*

7 Some girls under 13 use social media apps on their parents' phone. Icons/avatars should not be a child's face. Parents should follow, and keep checking privacy, location and safety settings of every device, app and social media website their child uses. Kids should not be in contact with anybody you don't know personally.

8 Parents need a record of all their kid's account names, PINs, and passwords for all email addresses, social media accounts and devices. Kids should always use the computer in a family part of the house.

9 A parent or guardian should be the only one to 'top up' phone credit or know any PIN numbers, and keep track of the usage.

10 All kids will strike problems online. Parents should aim for an attitude of calm, collaborative problem-solving, to encourage full disclosure.

11 More than an hour a day on screens and lack of outdoor play can cause eye damage and failure to develop proper long-distance sight. Too much screen time affects social skills and reduces time for sport, art, playing, daydreaming, being inventive and reading books.

12 All screen devices should be off an hour before bedtime. No wifi or screen devices, music players or TVs should be in kids' bedrooms overnight. All phones and other devices should be inaccessible all night, preferably in the parents' room.

13 All webcams should be disabled and covered with a piece of tape or plasticine so it can't be used by strangers to spy inside your house. Kids should use a mainstream product, such as Skype, to chat with only known friends, under supervision.

14 Parents need to tackle, not ignore, any online or phone bullying and if necessary get help and info from the relevant staff member at their kid's school.

15 See the More Info section for parents at the back of this book for more info about online and phone safety. And see the list of things kids need to know, coming up.

10 things kids need to know about phones, apps & being online

See the rules for parents on the previous page.

1 Anything that you post anywhere online, using an app, or on a phone you use, can possibly be seen by anybody. Don't post anything you wouldn't want your teachers, parents, grandparents and the rest of the world to see.

2 Never post any private information like your school, home address, phone number, birthday details, or info about your family. Strangers can use this to steal from your family or do you harm.

3 Ask your parents to help you to adjust 'privacy' and location settings on all phones and other devices. Never 'tag' any posts with a location or allow friends to tag you in photos. 'Don't allow' is your friend.

4 Know your own phone number and your parents' or guardians' phone numbers off by heart, even if they are stored in your phone.

Creeps online

You may think you're chatting online to a friend your own age but it might be a creepy adult man, pretending, instead. Creeps research bands, books, TV shows, movies, gaming, interactive websites and other stuff teenagers like, so they can sound younger. They use fake pictures. Their aim is to meet you or find out where you live, or watch you or keep talking to you, or sadly, to hurt you in some way.

They can be very cunning and patient, spending weeks or months turning you against friends and family; saying they're the only one who understands

5 Don't use any video apps or other social media apps or any other way of chatting live or posting video of yourself unless your parents help you do that.

6 Only allow friends you already know in 'real life' to have access to your posts. It doesn't matter how many 'followers' you have. What matters is who they are.

7 Don't have contact online or through your phone with anyone your parents don't know about.

8 Even as a joke, never send nude pictures or photos of yourself in underwear: it's illegal. You will lose control of who gets to see the pictures.

9 If any contact on social media or something you see online or on your phone seems wrong or makes you feel uncomfortable, tell your parents or your teacher.

10 Never, ever, *ever* go to meet somebody in real life that you have met online unless your parents come with you. It is rare, but some girls have been kidnapped and hurt by adult men who had been pretending to be their young friend.

you; telling untrue stories of illness or bullying to make you feel sorry for them; promising you money, exciting holidays or presents; making you believe they're a celeb or a friend, or somebody who loves you; or blackmailing you by threatening to tell your parents something bad or to hurt you or someone else.

Warning signs of a creep:
- Your parents don't know that person.
- The person wants to meet you in the 'real world'.
- They want you to send them photos or turn on your web cam.
- They want to give you a present, or money or credit.
- They want to keep your 'friendship' secret or private.
- They mention things or ask questions that don't seem okay.
- Sometimes they're nice and sometimes they seem threatening.

Tell a trusted adult straight away about any behaviour that seems a bit weird.

FACT

Scams Even if it seems okay, or a post or call says you could win a prize or some money or get game credits or time, *never* give your full name, date of birth, address, school or other including parents' credit card numbers or bank info to ANYONE online or on social media. This is always a scam to try and steal money.

FACT

Pic flick If an embarrassing pic of you is posted or texted, don't despair. Ask friends to delete it, get help from a trusted adult to work out how to stop it happening again, and put it down to experience. One picture doesn't define you.

'My phone was telling everyone where I was! My aunty fixed it.' **Aliyah**

Getting your independence online

The online and gaming world has some fun stuff. But it will all still be there – in fact there'll be better stuff there – when you turn 13 and as you get older. Even when it seems totally safe, it isn't. So enjoy lots of other stuff as well, and form a partnership with your parents about the responsibilities of being online. This way, when the time comes for you to have some more independence, they'll know you understand the risks and the rules.

'A girl in my year had embarrassing photos put online recently and nobody looks at her differently. Don't waste time regretting what happened, everyone makes mistakes, don't let them hold you back.'

Elle

PART 5
FEELING GOOD

11. Confidence 117
12. Moods & Emotions 126

judge yourself kindly

"Hey, I look nice"

11

CONFIDENCE

Confident people believe, 'I'm okay, and it doesn't really matter whether you agree.' Real cool has nothing to do with fashion or money or looking 'hot': it's about what's inside your head. Nobody expects you to have total confidence all at once. But it's something to work towards. The more you can laugh about things, the more that you don't obsess about what other people think, or how you appear to others, the freer and happier you'll be.

Not feeling confident

It can be hard to feel self-confident when you're approaching the teenage years because:

- Body changes might make you feel super-aware of yourself.
- You may want to blend in and not be noticed.
- It can be tough not caring about what other people say about you, even if you don't like them.
- You might be from a family that doesn't believe in praising you or celebrating your achievements and who you are.
- You're naturally shy or feel easily embarrassed (more on this coming up).

'Avoid negative thought patterns and remember life is what you make it, and not everything is always about you – no one is constantly taking notice of what you are doing.'

Freya

I'll have what she's having...

BRAND

do you want to hide, blend in, or stand out?

Stuff that gets in the way of confidence

Being shy

Lots of people are shy, even famous people. And that's okay. I hate it when somebody says, 'Don't be shy.' As if they'd ever say 'Don't have brown hair'! Being shy might just be a part of you. It's only a problem if you also feel nervous or upset: staying quiet until you warm up to new people is actually pretty smart. You can always dance on the table later. If you find shyness makes you miserable, ask a parent or a school counsellor for help.

Feeling embarrassed

By the time you get older you'll probably never be embarrassed and quite happy to go shopping in a hairnet, overcoat and socks with thongs, singing the National Anthem. (Or maybe that's just going to be me.) Approaching the teen years you might feel more self-aware and embarrassed more often – luckily it's usually a quick spiky feeling that's invisible to everyone else.

Blushing

One visible sign of embarrassment is blushing. This happens because stress can cause your blood to pump around faster, which makes you look redder. Probably nobody notices the blushing except you, but if it happens, breathe deeply in and out, and I promise it will fade.

'Don't listen to what people say, and don't believe the photos in magazines. Value you. Value what you have to offer to the world as a human being, not as a pretty face. No one else has the right to judge you for the importance or adequacy of your contribution to the world. And if they think they do, prove them wrong.' Nicola

How to feel more confident

Here are some steps on the way to feeling good about yourself and your strengths, talents and capabilities.

Get some basic body confidence

- Stand up and sit up straight (seriously – it makes you look more confident).
- Wear comfy clothes.
- Give yourself time to adjust to any new body changes. You will adjust and feel comfortable 'in your own skin'.

Encourage yourself

- Make a list of your good points (you don't have to show it to anyone else).
- What would you say to a friend to make her feel better? Tell it to yourself.
- Be still for a while. Sit or walk by yourself and give yourself time to think away from screens of any kind. Daydreaming and playing are important at your age. If anyone tells you to stop staring out the window, tell them I said you're developing your brain!

> 'When I was little I felt embarrassed about being different. Later I learned that the things that make you different make you special.'
> **Kylie Kwong, chef, author**

yay

everyone's BRAINY at something...

'Avoid negative thought patterns and remember life is what you make it, and not everything is always about you – no one is constantly taking notice of what you are doing.' **Yildiz**

confidence FEELING GOOD **121**

- You don't have to know everything. 'I don't know' is a perfectly fine answer to a lot of questions.
- Keep in mind that it doesn't matter if someone doesn't like you. Not everyone has to like you. Some people liking you is plenty.

Practise

- Try new things. As long as it's fun, give new sports, arts and hobbies a go, even if you're not good at them straight away.
- Don't worry about making mistakes. That's how you know you're learning. Mistakes are just an investment in a more confident future.
- Defy any labels or reputation put on you such as 'not smart' or 'mean'. Show with your behaviour that you can be your own person, no matter what's happened in the past.

Be assertive

'Assertive' means being able to stand up for yourself and what you believe in. It means being able to say no as well as yes. It means being able to make the right decision and act on it, even when the right decision isn't the easiest or most popular one. (It *doesn't* mean being loud and bossy or imposing yourself and your ideas on other people.) Ask trusted adults to listen to your problems and help you.

> 'When people say something nice to you appreciate it and take it on board because it makes you feel better about yourself. When you are having a bad day you can think about the things that are good about you.'
>
> Jessie

Some ways to say no:
- 'No.'
- 'Nup.'
- 'No thanks. It's not really my thing.'
- 'I'm pretty busy right now.'
- 'I'm not allowed.'
- I'll have to ask my mum/dad/guardian (and then get them to pretend they said no).
- 'I can't, sorry.'
- 'Maybe another time.'
- 'I've got too much on at the moment.'
- 'I'll let you know later/tomorrow/next week.' (This gives you time to think.)

Know your rights

Being confident means knowing your rights and being able to speak up, or tell somebody about it when those rights are violated (ignored). You have the right to feel safe. You have the right to an education. You have the right to community and school funding for sport, equal to that given to boys' sport. You have the right not to be touched by anyone else in any way that makes you feel uncomfortable. You have the right not to be harassed, or hit, or hurt. These are legal rights that all kids have, no matter what family or school they're in.

Girl power

Some people who aren't very smart think that girls aren't as good as boys, and that women aren't as good as men. Even some not-at-all-smart adults think this. In fact, girls and women are a mixture of strong and vulnerable, just like boys and men are. There is still so much discrimination against girls and women in the world.

Girls and women are more likely to be insulted (with mean, sexual or threatening comments), assaulted (physically hurt), paid less for the same job, allowed less power or education, given less respect, fewer jobs on TV and in politics, and lots of other places. Women everywhere still have to fight and argue for our rights.

'Feminism', 'women's rights' and 'girl power' are all different ways of saying the same thing: support for girls and women to have equal opportunities to boys and men.

Given the chance, women can be, and all over the world already *are* pilots, doctors, prime ministers, adventurers, electronic engineers, great mums, artists, oceanographers, scientists (see the list coming up), bridge builders, acrobats, soldiers, firefighters, farmers and anything else you can think of. Women can do any job a man can, except maybe be a professional willy-waver, and really, we so don't need any of those. So don't let anyone tell you that you can't do anything because you're a girl. There's a great big sisterhood of girls and women out here who want to support you and try to make sure you – and every girl in the world – is treated with the respect she deserves. In the meantime – stay strong, sister!

What some girls said they feel confident about*

my sporting ability ✽ **my morals and personality** ✽ my hair ✽ I'm good at acting so even if I don't FEEL confident I act as though I am ✽ I'm not bad looking; I know I can make people laugh; I can walk in heels ✽ **that I am a good person, that I am intelligent and healthy, and not too ugly** ✽ my friends ✽ speaking in front of my class mates! ✽ Um . . . everything basically ✽ not much ✽ nothing ✽ **my intelligence** ✽ being able to enjoy myself ✽ doing school work and playing sport ✽ drumming ✽ answering teachers' questions – sounds stupid, I know, but people think I do that well ✽ **outdoor stuff** ✽ that I can walk the streets at any time of day and feel that if I am attacked I will be able to defend myself ✽ I'm a good listener; I live to help friends and I'm confident that in some ways I can help ✽ **how I look when I am wearing clothes my mum says suit me** ✽ talking to people ✽ don't really feel confident about anything, I just love to give everything a go ✽ sports ✽ **my reading/writing ability; performing** ✽ nothing – but I can deal with nerves okay ✽ I try to look and feel confident about everything ✽ my image, my friends ✽ that I am going to be happy and successful in whatever path I choose to follow in my life ✽ my face ✽ **my family loving me no matter what** ✽ my swimming and my legs – love my legs! ✽ that I can look after myself and young children ✽ my personality and those who I can trust ✽ **my dancing** ✽ asking for assistance; talking to adults; ability to do well at school; trying new things ✽ people always say I'm a nice person ✽ **I can always make my friends laugh** ✽ I am good ✽ playing wing defence in netball, and making a fool of myself for a laugh ✽ my family loving me ✽

my life, and I am doing the best I can to live life to the fullest ✽ mixing with new and different people ✽ I'm not popular and I don't want to be so I can just be myself because my friends accept me for who I am ✽ **sailing, and having a laugh** ✽ art ✽ being around my friends and my family ✽ everything ✽ my calves ✽ my tae kwon do abilities ✽ wearing what I feel comfortable in ✽ my hair (sometimes) ✽ everything except public speaking and talking to guys ✽ **getting where I want to be** ✽ I have a larger vocabulary than my friends 'cause I like to read – this makes me feel special ✽ **who I am on the inside** ✽ I am good at netball and people like me (most of the time!) ✽ my fringe ✽ that I can talk to strangers now ✽ basically everything but my appearance ✽ **my attitude** ✽ the way I dance ✽ I'm a good friend ✽ schoolwork ✽ being gay ✽ **making new friends and not caring about what people think or say about me** ✽ everything – I'm an overly confident person ✽ cycling ✽ cooking, and standing up for my rights ✽ designing! ✽ **helping people sort out their problems** ✽ acting – it's when I can be a different character, not me any more! ✽ my intelligence ✽ my personality ✽ being myself; trying hard at everything ✽ **I am a good person** ✽ I'm able to hide my insecurities from myself and others so that I may be confident ✽ singing ✽ when I am in a group of people ✽ my mum – we have a good relationship ✽ **my image – I'm different and I like it** ✽ showing people the movies I make; talking to little kids ✽ my smile ✽ my clothes ✽ I feel that I am very good at science and I'm the best in my class ✽ I want to become a journalist and I'm confident that I will become one ✽ I feel confident when I am laughing ✽ karate and music and school ✽ **everything** ✽

✽ From the *Girl Stuff* book survey

12
MOODS & EMOTIONS

The combination of body and hormone changes mixed with events in your life and even the weather can combine to change your moods. In one afternoon you could feel proud, embarrassed, sad, happy, brave and slightly baffled. Not to mention giggly, creative, clever, annoyed, and dying to lie down in a hammock.

This chapter shows how to deal with negative thoughts and moods such as being worried, angry or embarrassed, and how to get through a time of sadness. Being a girl should include lots of fun and laughter. So just in case you need it, there's info on how to feel more cheerful, too.

Pick a mood, any mood

There are several possible reasons for feeling up and down and all over the place.

- You haven't had enough sleep – this can make you cranky.
- The levels of your brain's chemicals can get a bit out of whack temporarily, because of misbehaving hormones. This can make you feel more anxious.
- Changing moods can be a normal, even smart response to happy or sad things that happen that are out of your control.

Adults sometimes get cranky or start singing for no apparent reason, and you know that toddlers have epic tantrums – so don't let anyone tell you that moods are only for teenagers. Still, the combination of body and hormone changes, as well as events going on in your life, means that feeling moody can be a big part of being a girl. Having more awareness about your moods can help you to deal with them.

Anger

Everyone feels angry sometimes, maybe because something that seems unfair, or something that's out of your control. Anger needs to be expressed – talked through. Anger isn't helped by being violent, or sulking, or refusing to communicate. If you don't acknowledge and talk about your anger, it will still be there. Talking to someone who will listen is a good way to work out what's going on inside you. Sometimes you need to explain that you don't need a solution, you just want to talk it over.

Drawing, or writing down your thoughts and feelings can also help you recognise, understand and express your anger. Physical exercise like running or dancing can help you feel better.

Worry & stress

Everyone sometimes feels nervous, worried, concerned or scared about things that might or will happen.

Stress is more like the feeling of being out of control or concerned that you might not cope with something. Anxiety is more about being worried or nervous. (Anxiety is pronounced ang-zie-itty. The middle bit rhymes with pie.) But sometimes they just feel kind of the same.

These feelings can be 'all in the mind' or also cause physical things to happen like a headache or feeling squirgly in the stomach, being aware of your heart beating fast, tears springing to your eyes, sweating more than usual, and having trouble getting to sleep or waking up too early. You can get more colds and other illnesses because your body's too busy dealing with stress or anxiety to run a healthy immune system. (Anxious, by the way, is pronounced ang-shus.)

'You just hit "one of those days" and you're down for no apparent reason.' Danielle

Beating anxiety & stress

Here are some good ways to tackle feeling worried:

- Talk about your feelings with Mum, Dad, a grandparent, friends, your aunty, a doctor or nurse, a friend's mum, a counsellor or teacher, or anyone else you feel comfortable with. Some girls feel much better after they talk to their pets!
- Do some physical activity each day – it can help you be a calmer person. Some schools teach a technique called mindfulness, a way of thinking that can help.
- Breathe slowly – this is a quick, simple way of heading back towards calm. Breathe in gently and slowly for a count of 6 (or 4, or whatever you can manage). Pause, then breathe out gently and slowly for a count of 6, if you can. Repeat for a minute or so.

> 'I find sport the best way to relax and you can let all your anger and frustration out.'
> Ashleigh

If you feel panicked often, or feel that your anxiety seems out of control, or your inner thoughts are always negative, or you feel that you want to punish yourself, get Mum, Dad or a guardian to take you to the doctor, or to a school counsellor. There's lots of help available for helping you learn to get control of your stressful feelings.

Sadness

At the risk of being blindingly obvious, it's okay to feel sad sometimes even if you're not sure why. It's sometimes called 'feeling blue'. Almost everyone goes through bad patches, moody phases and feels down occasionally. Comparing a 'down' with an 'up' feeling is how we know the 'ups' are 'ups' and not 'sidewayses' – okay, that might not be an actual word.

> 'I'm sad when I am tired.' Lisa

Sadness can be a feeling of slight flatness or a 'low' after a big excitement has ended, it could last for a couple of days. You might have 'a good cry' because you feel a bit overwhelmed. If sadness becomes your usual mood no matter what happens, or you feel an ongoing depression or blankness, you need to reach out for help.

Grief

Bereavement and grief are words used to cover the intense feelings caused by a severe emotional loss, like a death in the family or your community; a family or relationship break-up; being a refugee or the victim of a crime; somebody leaving; or a serious illness.

Different people grieve in different ways and show it (or hide it) differently. Even those in the same family or a group who have the same reason for the grief can react to it very differently.

The swirling feelings of grief can include lots of responses, all normal, including crying, pretending it didn't happen, feeling angry, sadness, blankness (feeling 'nothing') asking questions that can never be answered, wondering if you caused it or made it happen, and feeling alone.

As well as these reactions, many grieving people experience physical symptoms, including headaches, an upset stomach, tiredness, trouble sleeping or sleeping too much.

Nobody should expect you just to 'get over it'. You need time to grieve properly, and then find a way to take your sadness with you into the next phase of your life where you can feel more positive, without having to forget someone or pretend an important event never happened.

See the section on feeling strong and optimistic, coming up.

'Don't say "It's too hard, nobody can help me." Try this: "It will get better, and I can help myself." If you admit to yourself you're on the way up, people can help again.' **Katie**

Feeling sad

People often say they're 'feeling a bit depressed', usually meaning they're feeling sad. Having or suffering from depression is different: it's a strong feeling of blankness or hopelessness that seems to go on and on: these feelings need to be treated by a doctor.

> 'Give yourself a reality check when you feel one comment or incident wearing you down. Mentally list 10 things that make you special, beautiful, different.'
>
> Chloe

bewildered... bewitched... bothered...

Sexual feelings

It's normal to have sexual feelings or be curious about sex way before you are interested in doing anything about it. And it's important to know about sex way before then anyway. You'll need to decide for yourself how that should happen – or not happen – how to stay safe and not get pregnant. For the time being, just be reassured that it's normal (*normal!*) to have romantic or sexual thoughts. You don't have to act on them. And it's just as normal (norrrrrmalllll!) not to have those feelings, too.

You'll probably hear lots of words and sly jokes about sex and maybe be shown images of sex on phones or other devices, usually by someone trying to embarrass you. Don't worry, that's not how sex really is for people. And it's not something everyone does when they have a boyfriend or girlfriend.

It's okay to say 'euww' and ignore any pictures or conversation about sex. And if it makes you feel uncomfortable tell a trusted adult about what's been happening. In fact, tell a trusted adult if *anything* is happening that makes you feel uncomfortable. The big-sister version of this book, **GIRL STUFF: Your Full-on Guide to the Teen Years** has much more about all emotional and physical aspects of sexuality. This includes how to say no, and what you need to know before you ever say yes (it's okay, you can wait until you are at least 36).

I'd rather stick a fork in my eye

You may not be interested in anything to do with sex

Feeling optimistic and strong

Some kids have the ability to 'bounce back' quickly after a bad patch, or feeling down for a bit. Some people are just optimistic at heart: they expect things will turn out okay. If that's not you, you'll be relieved to hear that you don't have to be born with optimism – you can learn it.

You can also learn to be a survivor who can face hard times and come through it all okay; the sort of person who can take a disappointment, instead of going off to brood for days or weeks.

'If my sister and me bake cookies together I forget my problems and have fun.'

Sara

'Stop stressing about the little things, believe me, you will get through it.' Kate

Top 10 ways to get strong

1 Be the person you want to be. If you try to be a good person then you can feel confident about yourself. When a bad thing happens you'll know it's not your fault.

2 Have a support team. It could be family or friends or both. Being part of a team, club or neighbourhood helps.

3 Have a go-to list of people, activities, movies, books and music that cheer you up (some lists and suggestions coming up).

4 Think about great times you've had. Think about bad times you went through that got better.

5 Don't make dramas or complain to everyone about little things. Save your energy to deal with real problems.

6 Try to be realistic. Instead of saying 'Nothing will ever change', set an achievable goal.

7 Stand your ground on getting help to fix the big things, even if they are not big to someone else.

8 Have breakfast and two other good meals every day; drink water when you're thirsty.

9 Recognise that sometimes things don't get better by themselves – you may have to take action or ask for help. Sometimes you have to be determined and persevere before things improve.

10 Reach out for support when you need it: this way you'll get more experienced at solving problems, feel braver, get to know yourself and be better prepared for obstacles in life.

Top 10 cheer-up hints

1 Laugh: with friends, at a movie or TV show. If necessary, get in a water or pillow "fight". See the lists of good movies and TV shows coming up.

2 Get lost: in the world of a good book – see the lists of great ones coming up.

3 Get out: into the fresh air and light – proven mood lifters.

4 Girls often focus on their weaknesses, the bits of themselves that 'need work' or 'could be better'. How about your strengths? Make a list in your head or on paper of your good points or achievements.

5 Explore: your creative side – express your feelings in writing, drawing, music, performance, cooking.

6 Schedule some fun. Make a date to look forward to with family or friends.

7 Take time out for yourself. Listen to some calm music, or have a dance while tidying up your room so it seems calm and uncluttered. Do some drawing and daydream at the same time.

8 Do a good deed. This could include helping to look after an animal, or volunteering some time or money at school to help a charity.

9 You choose whether to hang out with a pal, or on your own for a while. Some people want to spend every spare moment with other people, liking to be 'kept company', but others prefer to have some time on their own.

10 Sing. Even if you 'can't sing'. Get out into a paddock or under the shower and belt out a favourite song, or get a friend to do some karaoke with you.

'There are so many positive things . . . We meet new people, watch new movies, read new books, have new experiences every day.' **Amy**

fun lists

Part of the fun of getting older is finding new books, jokes, films and TV shows to enjoy. Here's a list of ones other girls love, and some heroines to admire. Add your own favourites to the lists!

fantastic BOOKS for gIRLS aged 8 to 12+

Ask a bookshop staff member or a librarian about what you might like and be ready for. Part of the fun of stories and books is talking about them with other fans! This list is arranged roughly in order of books for youngest to oldest (or the more advanced reader). Reading it makes me want to go and curl up in bed with a book right *now*.

1. ***Clarice Bean*** by Lauren Child: great characters, great illustrations, and lots of other books about Clarice to be had.

2. ***The Story of Tracy Beaker***, ***Vicky Angel***, ***The Worst Thing About My Sister*** and other books by Jacqueline Wilson: her much-loved stories often include themes of family break-ups and other realities.

3. ***Spud & Charli*** by Samantha Wheeler: a girl, a horse. And bats, I tell you.

4. ***Eight Keys*** by Suzanne LaFleur: Elise, who's 11, is getting bullied at school. But then she uncovers an amazing secret.

5. ***Violet Ink*** by Rebecca Westcott: an emotional book about sisters; also her books ***Dandelion Clocks*** and ***Five Things They Never Told Me***.

6. Any book by Kate DiCamillo: Maybe ***Flora and Ulysses*** or ***The Tale of Despereaux*** or ***Because of Winn-Dixie***.

7. ***Playing Beattie Bow*** by Ruth Park: a beautiful, vintage novel about a girl whose game causes her to go back in time to late 1800s Sydney.

8. ***Withering by Sea*** by Judith Rossell: a multi-award-winning Victoria-era historical adventure with gorgeous illustrations.

Fun Lists 137

9 ***Anne of Green Gables*** by Lucy Maud Montgomery: an old classic with a girl heroine. More than 50 million copies have been sold in about 100 years.

10 ***The Secret Garden*** by Frances Hodgson Burnett: a 10-year-old orphan sent to live with a distant English uncle finds a secret garden, and a reason to be kind.

11 ***The Princess Diaries*** by Meg Cabot: how to keep your head when you accidentally become a princess.

12 ***Wonder*** by R.J. Palacio: a much-adored book about Auggie, a boy with a confronting facial abnormality who goes to a new primary school. How will he survive? Warning: you'll need tissues!

13 ***Flawd: How to Stop Hating on Yourself, Others, and the Things That Make You Who You Are*** by Emily-Anne Rigal: stories by real girls and reminiscing celebs. A great book for anyone struggling with self-esteem issues, having a hard time feeling different or up against meanness.

14 ***Through My Eyes***: series edited by Lyn White. Stories about kids in modern conflict zones: includes ***Shahana*** (by Rosanne Hawke), ***Amina*** (by J.L. Powers).

15 ***Matilda*** by Roald Dahl: an absolute classic about love, reading, and truly terrible parents.

16 ***Birrung the Secret Friend*** by Jackie French: one of Ms French's stories based on Australia's real history.

favourite book series for girls aged 8 to 12+

Ask your school librarian, local bookshop staff member, or author's website to help you find out which book is the first in the series. Otherwise you'll have the horrible experience of having to go backwards! Many of these series are also available as audiobooks for long journeys or while hiding under your bed. And check to see if your fave series has been made into a movie.

These books are arranged so the ones more suitable for older girls are furthest down the list.

1. The **Ruby Redfort** series by Lauren Child: a cranky but fun girl detective's adventures by the creator of *Clarice Bean*.

2. **Judy Moody** books by Megan McDonald: a series of stories starring the same lively, lovable heroine.

3. The **Molly Moon** series by Georgia Byng: Molly's fab, and also incidentally 'an orphan, a time traveler, master hypnotist, mind reader, and star'.

4. The **Alice-Miranda** series by Jacqueline Harvey: an upbeat posh girl's 'really quite lovely adventures'.

5. The **Ottoline** books and the **Goth Girl** series by Chris Riddell: splendid illustrations and fun stories about feisty girls.

6. **Our Australian Girl** collection: Aussie girls of different ethnic backgrounds from various times in history. A charm bracelet on the cover tells you the year, the main character, a theme, and its number in the series for that character.

7 **The Chronicles of Narnia** series by C.S. Lewis: you'll be amazed at what's at the back of the wardrobe and that it can last 7 books. *The Lion, the Witch and the Wardrobe* classic fantasy series.

8 **School for Good and Evil** by Soman Chainani: a fantasy trilogy based around said school, and best pals Agatha and Sophie. 'A world without princes' is a slogan to love.

9 **Little Women,** a classic, 4-book series by Louisa May Alcott: set in the early 1800s, with universal themes of love, independence and struggle.

10 **The Legend of Little Fur** series by Isobelle Carmody: a little elf-troll is central to 4 books full of friendship and adventure.

11 **The Immortals** series by Tamora Pierce: 4-book set featuring the adventures of magic heroine, a girl called Daine, in a medieval world.

12 **His Dark Materials** trilogy by Philip Pullman: absorbing fantasy world on a parallel earth, encompassing polar bears, fibbers, and daemons.

13 **The Deltora Quest** series and companion books by Emily Rodda: thrilling monsters, dragons, a fair bit of forest-based journeying and lots of imaginative creatures and characters.

14 **The Medusa Project** by Sophie McKenzie: 6-part adventure thriller about teen psychic crime-fighters.

great movies for girls aged 8 to 12+

Of course, everyone's different and scared or confused by different things in movies, so the choice of what to watch is up to you and your parents. These films are arranged roughly in order of suitability from 8 to 13 years old.

1. **Ferris Bueller's Day Off**: running away – from school and responsibilities.

2. **Freaky Friday**: a girl and a mum switch bodies.

3. **Despicable Me**: one of those animated families that thinks its normal. With their underground lair, and all.

4. **Inside Out**: feelings come to life in this sad, happy, clever movie voiced by great comedians, including Amy Poehler.

5. **Hairspray**: 1950s compassionate dance-fest romp.

6. **Mean Girls**: funny, wise and true about friends and frenemies.

7. **Muriel's Wedding**: Aussie classic about friends, love, & confidence.

8. **A League of Their Own**: the season of a women's baseball team.

9. **Lemony Snicket's A Series of Unfortunate Events**: fun suspense.

10. **Ella Enchanted**: boring princess fantasy twisted into a great comedy.

11 ***Kiki's Delivery Service***: a 13-year-old uses her powers for good.

12 ***Bend it Like Beckham***: the English daughter of Indian immigrants learns to become a soccer champion and a good friend.

13 ***The Wizard of Oz***: an old classic movie with admittedly alarming flying monkeys.

14 ***Pitch Perfect 1 & 2****:* the adventures of an a cappella singing group.

15 ***Labyrinth***: an imaginative extravaganza with creatures (and Muppets).

16 ***Girl Rising***: a documentary about girls around the world.

17 ***Dixie Chicks: Shut Up and Sing***: a true story about musicians & free speech.

18 ***Somewhere Between***: documentary about Chinese girls who have been adopted into American families.

19 ***The Chronicles of Narnia***: based on *The Lion the Witch and the Wardrobe* book.

20 ***Clueless***: irresistible remake of Jane Austen's *Emma* set in 1990s LA.

21 ***Rabbit-Proof Fence***: intense historical drama about Aboriginal girls who were taken from their family because of racist policies.

22 ***Whale Rider***: a family drama about future Moari leader Pai and how she comes to terms with her birthright and her independence.

Women Leaders in Science, Technology, Maths & Engineering

When you hear somebody say girls aren't good at maths or science, make them read this list out loud! These women represent just a tiny few of Australia's mathematicians, engineers, tech-head leaders and scientists, plus a handful of early pioneers.

Kirsti Abbott, ant enthusiast, ecologist ✤ **Yassmin Abdel-Magied**, engineer ✤ **Professor Katie Allen**, paediatric allergist and paediatrician ✤ **Robyn Arianhrod**, mathematician ✤ **Rao Asha**, mathematician ✤ **Professor Lynn Beazley**, neuroscientist ✤ **Emma Beckett**, biomedical research, food science ✤ **Dr Elena Belousova**, evolutionary metallurgy ✤ **Kathy Belov**, comparative genomics, Tassie devil specialist ✤ **Julie Bernhardt**, clinician, stroke specialist ✤ **Professor Christine Bigby**, social sciences, disability inclusion ✤ **Elizabeth Blackburn**, biological researcher, telomere expert, Nobel Prize winner ✤ **Nikola Bowden**, geneticist ✤ **Linda Broome**, zoologist ✤ **Dr Emma Burrows**, behavioural neuroscience ✤ **Mary Butler**, microbiologist ✤ **Maria Byrne**, marine scientist ✤ **Christine Chen**, defence engineer ✤ **Marita Cheng**, founder of Robogals, engineer ✤ **Margaret Clayton**, marine scientist ✤ **Ass. Prof. Lyn Corcoran**, molecular immunologist, lab head ✤ **Professor Suzanne Cory**, molecular biologist ✤ **Rachael Cox**, energy engineer ✤ **Clio Cresswell**, mathematician ✤ **Mahanda Dasgupta**, nuclear physicist ✤ **Upulie Divisekera**, molecular biologist, astro-paleontologist ✤ **Jane Elith**, bio-scientist ✤ **Dr Nicky Eshtiaghi**, chemical engineer ✤ **Dr Bronwyn Evans**, engineer, CEO ✤ **Dr Cathy Foley**, physicist, leader in materials science & engineering ✤ **Marilyn Fox**, biologist ✤ **Dr Margeurite Galea**, gene and cell specialist ✤ **Michelle Gallaher**, orthoptics, biotech ✤ **Professor Jenny Graves**, geneticist ✤ **Margaret Hamer**, first woman graduate aeronautical engineering, 1948 ✤ **Dr Maggie Hardy**, biochemist, entymologist ✤ **Jenna Haverfield**, reproductive research ✤ **Ass. Prof. Bronwyn Hemsley**, speech pathologist ✤ **Dorothy Hill**, geologist and paleontologist, first female professor in Australia (1960) ✤ **Kate Hoy**, clinical neuropsychologist ✤ **Dr Jodie Ingles**, geneticist ✤

Muireann Irish, cognitive neuroscientist ✤ **Misty Jenkins**, biomedical research specialist ✤ **Nalini Joshi**, mathematician ✤ **Ass. Prof. Katherine Kedzierska**, immunology researcher ✤ **Ass. Prof. Virginia Kilborn**, astrophysicist ✤ **Amy Kimball**, astronomer ✤ **Priscilla Kincaid Smith**, nephrologist ✤ **Georgina King**, pioneering geologist and anthropologist ✤ **Nuria Lorente**, astronomer ✤ **Lush Dora**, early bacteriologist, died of scrub typhus after needle-stick injury in the laboratory, 1943 ✤ **Katie Mack**, theoretical astrophysicist ✤ **Ruth MacKinnon**, luekaemia molecular researcher ✤ **Sarah Maddison**, astrophysicist ✤ **Wirginia Maixner**, neurosurgeon ✤ **Dr Francine Marques**, cardiovascular research ✤ **Professor Jenny Martin**, molecular bio-scientist ✤ **Isabel McBryde**, archeologist ✤ **Professor Angela Moles**, ecologist, botanist ✤ **Tanya Monro**, photonics physicist ✤ **Giang Nguyen**, mathematician ✤ **Tich-Lam Nguyen**, nanotechnologist ✤ **Alicia Oshlack**, bioinformatician ✤ **Ruby Payne Scott**, radio astronomy and physics pioneer ✤ **Professor Anne Penfold Street**, mathematician, educator ✤ **Sarah Perk-Kirk**, climate scientist ✤ **Professor Cheryl Praeger**, mathematician ✤ **Julie Preston**, microbiologist ✤ **Professor Emma Johnson**, marine ecologist, eco-toxoligist ✤ **Phyllis Rowntree**, pioneering bacteriologist ✤ **Jodi Rummer**, fish fancier, biodiversity expert ✤ **Emma Ryan-Weber**, astronomer ✤ **Veena Sahajwalla**, materials engineer, inventor ✤ **Professor Ingrid Scheffer**, paediatric neurologist ✤ **Professor Jennifer Seberry**, mathematician, computer scientist ✤ **Diana Shelstad**, mathematician ✤ **Else Shepherd**, electrical engineer ✤ **Professor Michelle Simmons**, quantum computing physicist ✤ **Dr Alicia Spittle**, physiotherapist, researcher ✤ **Fiona Stanley**, epidemiologist ✤ **Marie Stoner**, inventor, scientist ✤ **Dr Andrea Taschetto**, climate scientist ✤ **Dr Mel Thompson**, medical researcher, bacteriologist ✤ **Professor Marika Tiggeman**, social psychologist ✤ **Winifred Waddell**, botanist ✤ **Di Walker**, marine scientist ✤ **Leonie Walsh**, lead government scientist ✤ **Professor Rachel Webster**, astrophysicist ✤ **Margaret Wertheim**, mathematician, science writer, crocheted coral reef expert ✤ **Mary Williams**, pathologist ✤ **Dr Alice Williamson**, chemistry, malaria researcher ✤ **Dr Rachel Wilson**, research methodologist ✤ **Fiona Wood**, inventor, doctor ✤ **Giovanna Zanardo**, astrophysicist, astro-structuralist engineer ✤ **Astrid Zeman**, cognitive scientist.

Real-Life Heroines

5 real women we admire

Good on you and thank you:

* Malala Youssuf: fights for girls' rights and education.
* Tavi Gevinson: founder of Rookie.com.
* Taylor Swift: writes and sings her own feelings.
* Ellyse Perry: elite athlete in more than one code.
* Tarenorerer (Walyer): Tasmanian Aboriginal warrior. Survivor of kidnapping and slavery.

fill in your own:

----

fictitious Heroines

3 tippety-top fictitious heroines we love

We still love you even if you're not real:

* Pippi Longstocking of her own books by Astrid Lindgren: she lifts.
* Lisa Simpson: she rocks.
* Hermione Granger from the Harry Potter series: she thinks.

fill in your own:

Fun Lists

Lists

Fun Lists

Notes

148   Fun Lists

Your Doodles

DREAMS

Things to See

Fun Lists 151

Places to go →

IDEAS

Fun Lists 153

Adventures

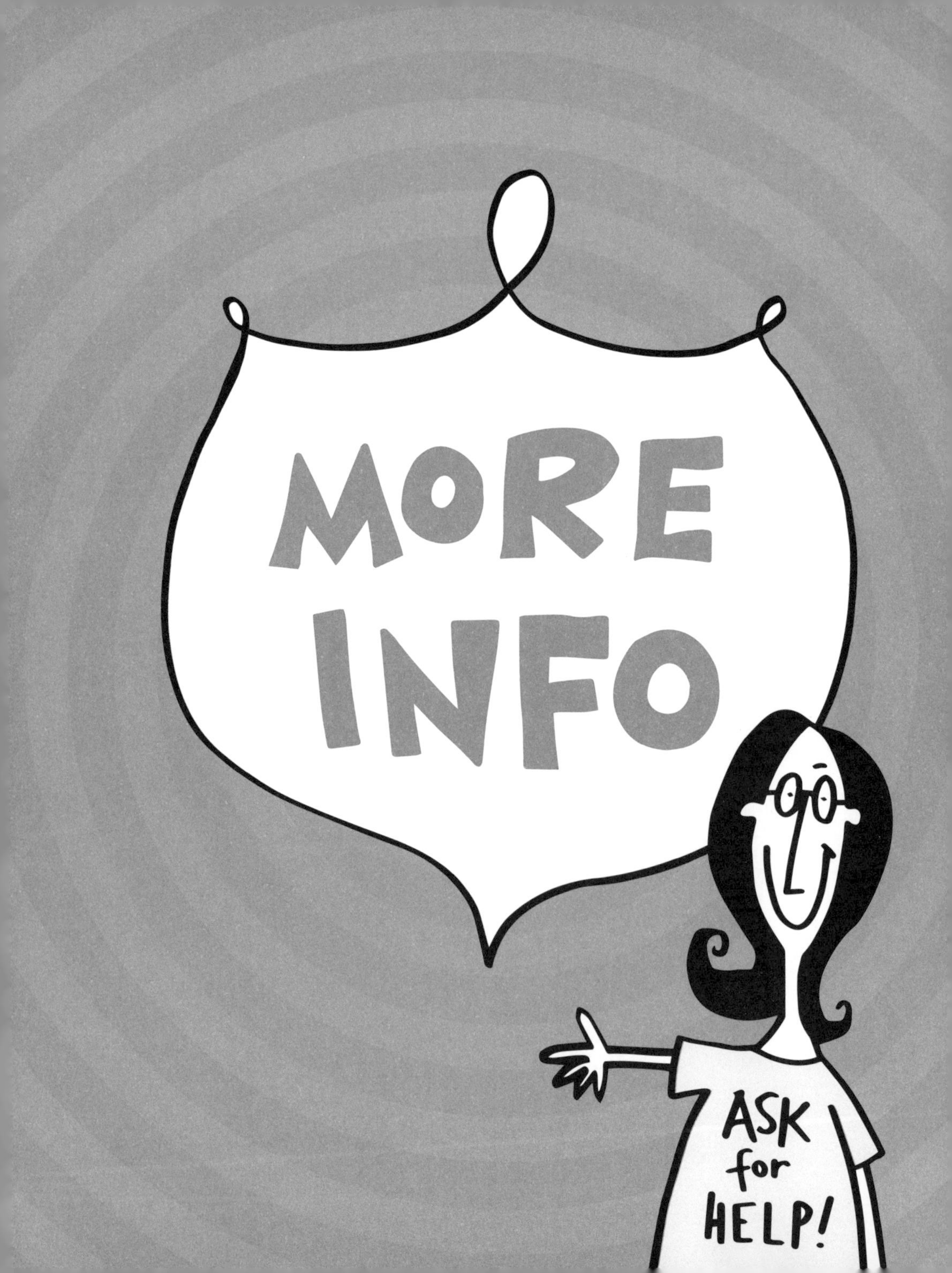
MORE INFO
ASK for HELP!

Helplines

Call these numbers in your country for help about any worry, anytime:

Kidsline Australia: 1800 55 1800

🥝 Kidsline New Zealand: 0800 543 754

Great websites for girls aged 8+

itwixie.com
Moderated, feel-good US site.

tweentribune.com
Online magazine for kids of various ages produced by American teachers.

sciencenewsforkids.org
Non-profit US science site.

australiangeographic.com.au
The archive of Australia's environmental magazine with pics & articles.

clubpenguin.com
A moderated, commercial Disney company site with an online community of mostly kids aged 6 to 12 in a virtual-reality game. Each player is represented by a penguin. You can join for free but you can also pay for extra features: don't try this without your parents' agreement and supervision!

Check whether what's on these sites is suitable for your age group:

onegirl.org.au
Charity dedicated to educating girls worldwide.

rosierespect.org.au
Wonderful Australian website for girls by non-profit women's organisations The Victorian Women's Trust & the Dugdale Trust for Women and Girls.

amysmartgirls.com
Founded by comedian Amy Poehler & her pal, focused on videos, images and messages and encouraging fun, caring & good self-esteem.

rookiemag.com
Tavi Gevinsson's brainchild, written by & for young women and girls.

More Info for Parents

Good sources of girl-friendly info include your family doctor (GP), and a community health centre or a school nurse if you're lucky enough to have one. Most websites with info for teens and pre-teens are by commercial interests so their info is biased to sell you something. The go-to websites I've chosen here tend to be independent sites.

For good ideas for presents of age-appropriate books and movies for girls aged 8 to 12, see the lists a few pages back.

Unless an entry has a little Kiwi next to it, which means New Zealand only all details are Australian unless otherwise stated.

Body Changes & Puberty

likeitis.org.au
Website with info about puberty & periods: interactive girly-bits diagram; heaps of Q&A.

shfpa.org.au
From the Sexual Health and Family Planning Australia main page choose your state or territory to find your nearest clinic; or for info call the FPA Healthline: 1300 658 886.

🥝 NZ government Healthline: 0800 611 116
Qualified nurses can answer your questions.

🥝 familyplanning.org.nz
Family Planning Association NZ. From the main page choose Find a Clinic.

Skin & Hair

dermcoll.asn.au
Dermatologists are doctors with an extra 5 years of training in skin and hair. You'll need a referral from your GP. This is the Australasian College of Dermatologists site: choose Public, then A–Z of Skin.

facial differences

youngwomenshealth.org

iface.org.uk
These offshore sites have lots of positive info on facial differences such as birthmarks or scars.

Sunscreen

sunsmart.com.au
The go-to Aussie site with good info on sunscreens, skin care & skin cancer in young people.
Advice line: 13 11 20.

sunsmart.co.nz
The official NZ site for sun info.

Bullying

amf.org.au
The Alannah and Madeleine Foundation runs the eSmart Schools Program: get your school involved.

bullyingnoway.gov.au
Info and resources to help with bullying issues, online or not.

Online & Phone Safety

Sexts, Texts and Selfies: How to Keep Your Child Safe in the Digital Space by Susan McLean, Australian expert. Really useful, clear book sprinkled with real, surprising case studies that cover creeps online, bullying & gaming addiction. Plus handy online safety 'contracts' for parents and kids.

Self-esteem & Identity

bornthiswayfoundation.org
Lady Gaga's global foundation to fight bullying. Stories of bravery.

igba.org.au and **itgetsbetter.org**
A local and global video project with reassuring messages about being gay.

reach.org.au
The Reach organisation offers workshops for schools & community groups on body image and self-esteem.

Girl Power

everydaysexism.com
Women contribute everyday stories and incidents.

ywca.org.au
🥝 **ywca.org.nz**
National HQs for the YWCA which is run by and for women and girls, with all sorts of useful programs and campaigns.

Other useful women's organisations include **cwaa.org.au** (Country Women's Association), **finallyfeminism101.wordpress.com** (for Q&As about women's rights); and **globalfundforwomen.org** (projects to help women and girls worldwide).

General Health

immunise.health.gov.au
Info line 1800 671 811

Girls should be up to date on the Australian childhood immunisation schedule, & between the age of 10 and 13 they need a series of 3 'jabs' to protect against cervical cancers. If these are given at school, you won't need to pay for them at a doctor's clinic.

healthinsite.gov.au

An A–Z list of illnesses & conditions with trusted medical info.

wwda.org.au

Women With Disabilities Australia site.

thewomens.org.au

The Royal Women's Hospital of Melbourne has good fact sheets on various health issues.

Food

marketfresh.com.au

Info on what's in season (and therefore cheaper) & fun ways to cook or serve fruit and vegies.

choice.com.au

On the Australian Consumers' Association home page search Breakfast Cereals, Fast Food or Food, School Lunches, or whatever else ye fancy.

foodstandards.gov.au

Choose Food Consumer Information then Labelling. You can download a poster, 'Food Labels: What Do They Mean?'.

Positive eating behaviours

thebutterflyfoundation.org.au
Info and support for families about eating behaviours & disorders.

daa.asn.au
The Dietitians Association of Australia has articles on nutrition & recipes and can help you find a specialist dietician. (Anyone can call themselves a nutritionist – a dietician has a medically recognised university qualification.)

haescommunity.org
A physiologist with a specialty in weight issues promotes Health At Every Size (HAES): info and support for self-acceptance.

about-face.org
Questions negative and demeaning images of women in society.

bodypositive.com
Two US sites about feeling better in yourself.

ifnotdieting.com.au
Dr Rick Kausman offers calming, useful ideas and a healthy approach to food & self-image.

Food allergies & intolerances

allergyfacts.org.au
Anaphylaxis Australia's site has info, advice & support for serious allergies.

coeliac.com.au
Also for people with gluten and lactose intolerance, fructose malabsorption and irritable bowel syndrome (IBS): info, support & links from specialist Australian dietician Dr Sue Shepherd.

family problems

1800respect.org.au
24-hour phone counselling 1800 737 732
For help, support & info about controlling relationships, family violence, sexual assault or intimidation.

relationships.org.au
Relationships Australia can help you find courses in parenting, relationships, and anger management. Call 1300 364 277.

grief

grief.org.au
Inquiries: 1300 664 786
Help to find a counsellor.

reachout.com
Choose Tough Times then Loss and Grief for fact sheets, real stories & help.

nalag.org.au
🥝 **nalag.org.nz**
Referrals to a grief counsellor or support group, or help with ideas for a ritual or ceremony from the National Association For Loss & Grief.

movies, apps & websites

commonsensemedia.org
A non-profit independent American site with sensible info about age-appropriate games, apps, websites etc.

childrenandmedia.org.au
Australian Council on Children and the Media's non-profit site with reviews for parents.

Hey, Girl!

That's the end of the book... Want more?

The big-sister version of this book
Girl Stuff: Your Full-on Guide to the Teen Years has more!

GIRL STUFF

Your full-on guide to the teen years

GIRL STUFF: Your Full-on Guide to the Teen Years, for girls aged 12 to 18, has more on all this:

LOVE

BODY IMAGE

you look **FINE**, girl

DRINKING

going to throw up...

Be your own best friend

FAMILY

RULES
1. no undies on heads
2. feed the ferret

CLOTHES

rummage, rummage...

MENTAL HEALTH

SEX

MAKE-UP

um....

Remind me again - what's the point?

DRUGS

MORE ➡

GIRL STUFF: Your Full-on Guide to the Teen Years, for girls aged 12 to 18, has more on all this:

EATING

"Look after yourself."

SCHOOL

EXERCISE

walk to meet friends...

MONEY

SLEEP

Lack of sleep can make you ⸗CRANKY⸗

GIRLPOWER

I AM NOT a BOY TOY

MAKING A DIFFERENCE

Can I help you?

the environment

Acknowledgements

For this book I drew on the contributions of all the girls, other experts and consultants who helped with the latest edition of the original book, GIRL STUFF: **Your Full-on Guide to the Teen Years**.

Julie Gibbs was the original commissioning publisher and a great supporter and facilitator of all things *Girl Stuff*. Special thanks for the GIRL STUFF 8-12 edition are due to Kristin Otto (for the idea), Rachel Scully and Clementine Edwards (editery) (I wonder if they'll change that), Anyez Lindop (publicising), Adam Laszczuk (book design), Susan McClean (online and phones), Kristin Gill (for being generally ace plus books info), Dr Rod Phillips (skin), Neil Branch (Federal Health Departmentery), Susan Carland (expertery), Ben Ball (striding about and saying 'yes' as required), the staff of Post Pre-Press Typesetters in Queensland (typesetting whizzbangery), Kevin Whyte and Georgina Ogilvie (general whirlery). And especially Jude, Ciara, Molly, Poppy, Alannah, Jen, Alicia, Harriet and Vi for book and movie suggestions.

Relevant consultants for the original *Girl Stuff* and its continuing updates included more than 4000 girls who answered an online survey, original researcher Emma Moss, and adolescent specialist Professor Susan Sawyer. Dermatology consultants: Tanya Gilmour, Josie Yeatman, Belinda Welsh, Ruth Morley. Drugs consultant: Paul Dillon of Drug and Alcohol Research and Training Australia, school visitor extraordinaire. Mental health consultants: Dr Louise Newman, Monica Hadges, Dr Jayashri Kulkarni. Online consultant: Michelle Blanchard. Food consultants: Maureen Humphrey, clinical specialist, Dr Rick Kausman, Dr Zoe McCallum, specialist nurse Stephanie Campbell. Activity consultant: Dr Geraldine Naughton. Puberty and reproductive health consultants: Dr Melissa Cameron, Dr Susan Bagshaw, Annie Rose, Donna Tilley, Angela Steele. Psychologist consultants: Lorraine Rose, Antony Gleeson and Dr Helen McGrath. For a full list of consultants for each edition, see the big-sister book GIRL STUFF: **Your Full-on Guide to the Teen Years**.

Kaz Cooke is an Australian author, a mum, and a former girl.
She began her career as a reporter, sashayed into cartooning,
and has written several bestselling books including the
multi-award winning *Girl Stuff: Your Full-on Guide to the Teen Years*,
for which over 4000 girls contributed their thoughts and questions.
Her other books include *Up The Duff*, *Kidwrangling*,
The Terrible Underpants and *Wanda-Linda Goes Berserk*.
Kaz is a rabid feminist who enjoys toast and
dancing on the couch.

kazcooke.com.au

VIKING

UK | USA | Canada | Ireland | Australia
India | New Zealand | South Africa | China

Penguin Books is part of the Penguin Random House group of companies whose addresses can be found at global.penguinrandomhouse.com.

Penguin Random House Australia

First published by Penguin Group (Australia), 2016
Adapted in part from *Girl Stuff*, first published 2007

Text and illustrations copyright © Kaz Cooke 2007, 2016

The moral right of the author has been asserted.

All rights reserved. Without limiting the rights under copyright reserved above, no part of this publication may be reproduced, stored in or introduced into a retrieval system, or transmitted, in any form or by any means (electronic, mechanical, photocopying, recording or otherwise), without the prior written permission of both the copyright owner and the above publisher of this book.

Designed by Adam Laszczuk © Penguin Group (Australia)
Typeset in Stone Serif by Adam Laszczuk, Penguin Design Studio
Colour separation by Splitting Image Colour Studio, Clayton, Victoria
Printed in China by RR Donnelley Asia Printing Solutions Limited.

National Library of Australia
Cataloguing-in-Publication data:

> Cooke, Kaz, 1962– author.
> Girl stuff 8–12 / Kaz Cooke
> 9780143573999 (paperback)
> Preteen girls.
> Puberty
> Girls–Conduct of life.

305.234

penguin.com.au